SCHOOL OF
PRAYER

Time for a Revolution!

CANDY THOMAS

WESTBOW
PRESS
A DIVISION OF THOMAS NELSON
& ZONDERVAN

WestBow Press books may be ordered through booksellers or by contacting:

WestBow Press
A Division of Thomas Nelson & Zondervan
1663 Liberty Drive
Bloomington, IN 47403
www.westbowpress.com
1 (866) 928-1240

ISBN: 978-1-4908-8288-8 (sc)
ISBN: 978-1-4908-8289-5 (hc)
ISBN: 978-1-4908-8287-1 (e)

Library of Congress Control Number: 2015909006

Print information available on the last page.

WestBow Press rev. date: 07/10/2015

CONTENTS

PART FOUR: HAVING EARS TO HEAR

PART FIVE: WHILE YOU WAIT

DEDICATION

irst and foremost to my loving Savior and King, the Lord Jesus Christ, who most influenced this. To Him be all glory, honor, and praise forevermore.

To my beloved mother, Lillie Belle Lyles. The prayers of a mother are like no other! Mommy, although you went to be with the Lord on July 13, 2014, your godly example and unconditional love are still shaping my life in a way that will last all my days. You are forever in my heart.

To my husband, Jeffery. Your support and understanding were an important source of encouragement to me from start to finish. You are the biggest dreamer I've ever known, and you teach me by example every day how to persevere when battling challenges and how to never give up.

To my wonderful children, Jeffrey, Teresa, Cameron, and Stephanie. You cheer me on in whatever I attempt to do, and your unconditional love gives me added strength. Each one of you is God's very special blessing to me, and being your mother will always remain the most fulfilling assignment of my life.

To my siblings, Dee, Retta, Robert, Al, and Cindy. Each of you in your own special way reminded me it's never too late to go for your dreams. You've been there for me when I needed you, praying, giving financial support, providing a well-timed "You *go*, girl!", or using your influence to create new opportunities for me to use my gifts.

To countless precious brothers and sisters in Christ. There are too many of you to name, but I want you to know I greatly appreciate you for your support especially during those years when I was struggling to find God's will for my life. Thank you for your prayers and the loving acts of kindness shown. They will never be forgotten.

My prayer

> Lord, please bless each one abundantly. Give them a hundredfold return for every act of kindness or generosity that was shown to me in Your name. I ask this in the name of Jesus. Amen.

INTRODUCTION

This may seem odd, but I felt led to begin with the following disclaimer: Let it be known that if you are not a believer in Jesus Christ as the only begotten Son of God and the only way to the Father, this book will make very little sense to you. As a matter of fact, it will probably sound like a bunch of foolishness to you because much of what it contains is of a spiritual nature.

The Bible says things that come from the Spirit of God can only be discerned through the Spirit. However, Christianity is not a mystical society or Bible book club. We're the family of God, and He's reaching out to the whole world through us, telling all men everywhere that all it takes to become His child is to believe in Jesus Christ as His Son with your heart and confess Him with your mouth.

That being said, it's only reasonable that a book on prayer would begin with the most important prayer that any person could ever pray: a prayer to receive Christ. So I want to give you that opportunity, right now. If you want to know God and receive forgiveness for your sin, pray the following prayer out loud and mean it with all your heart. If you are sincere, God will hear you and answer your prayer.

> Dear holy Lord, I admit I am separated from You by
> my sin, and I am lost without You. I believe that You
> still loved me so much that thousands of years ago,
> You sent Jesus, Your Son, to die for me in payment

of my sin debt. I believe He rose back to life from the dead in victory over sin and death. I now turn away from sin and invite Jesus into my heart. Thank You for forgiving me. I am washed clean and set free from sin, right now. I receive Your Holy Spirit into my inner being, enabling me to walk in Your power and to spiritually communicate with You in prayer. Thank You for my new life in Christ beginning this very instant. Amen.

Awesome! Congratulations and welcome to the family of God! Now we have something to work with! As a new believer, it's very important to confess Christ by telling someone what happened to you. Let them know that you received Christ as your Savior and you got born again. Now that you have access to God, ask Him to lead you to a good church, because the next step in your walk with Christ is to get connected with other believers ASAP. Tell the church you want to get baptized. They will help you learn how to study the Bible, so you can grow spiritually.

You are a part of God's family now, and as with any family, there are both privileges and responsibilities. We need each other; we are one spiritual body in Christ, and He is our head.

While you are waiting to find the right church, start reading the Bible. The New Testament book of John is a great place to start to learn who Jesus is. The first three chapters of Genesis will explain the creation story. The Psalms and Proverbs provide a wonderful source of wisdom. The other books of the New Testament will help you understand what it means to be a Christian and help you gain the right perspective on what it means to have a relationship with God by grace under the new covenant. It is important to understand the foundational truths of the New Testament before trying to tackle the Old Testament.

I don't recommend this book as a speed-reading project. To get the most out of it, please read it slowly. Don't worry if some things seem a little hard to understand at first. It will begin to make more sense as you grow in your relationship with the Holy Spirit.

To those of you who are already believers, please answer these questions before you decide if reading this book will be worth your while. Try your best to answer them honestly.

1. How important is prayer to you on a scale of 1 to 10?
2. If your number is close to 10, do you take absolutely everything in your life to God in prayer or just what is problematic?
3. Have you ever been in your prayer time and had trouble "getting through"?
4. How confident are you in prayers that God will answer them?
5. What do you do when it feels like your prayers hit the ceiling and come crashing back down on your head?
6. Do you believe God still does miracles, today?
7. Have you ever prayed for a big miracle for yourself or anyone else?
8. Have you ever given up on expecting a miracle?
9. If you did give up on a miracle, what caused you to give up?
10. Did your giving up change your belief about miracles or prayer?
11. How do you react when you don't receive either a "yes" or "no" answer to a prayer if you need an answer right away?
12. When you feel reasonably confident that God said yes to a prayer request, but you don't see any manifestation of your answer, what do you do next?
13. How do you respond when you know for sure God's answer is no?

Now that you've allowed yourself to be a bit honest, take a little self-test to gauge your prayer aptitude. How do you tend to respond to the following situations?

1. Someone asks you to pray for an important need they have.
   a) I say I will and make a mental note to pray for them later.
   b) I ask for more specifics and pray with them right then and there.
2. You're in the middle of an emotionally charged situation.
   a) I respond emotionally first, then have to pray later on how to fix my hasty reaction.
   b) I keep my peace, pray, and then respond later based on God's wisdom.
3. You have to make a very important decision.
   a) I seek wisdom from others first, then pray about which is the best advice to take.
   b) I seek wisdom from God in prayer first, delaying action until I hear from Him.

Okay. Now grade yourself. Well, how'd you do? If you gave honest answers, rather than what you thought was a good Christian answer, your responses revealed your prayer aptitude. In other words, it showed how central prayer is to you in everyday life.

> Perfect = "I chose number 2 for all my responses because I already have this prayer stuff totally under control. Thanks, but no thanks. I don't think there's anything new I can learn from this book."
> Need improvement = "All my responses weren't number 2's. I think I'll keep reading."

If you graded yourself "perfect," praise the Lord! Maybe you should ask the Lord if He wants you to write a book on prayer, start a new Bible study on prayer, or increase your support for prayer meetings at your church to help others get where you are. The need for prayer is plentiful, but the prayers are few, so go for it!

However, if you graded yourself "need improvement," don't beat up on yourself; congratulate yourself for being so honest. I have a few things the Spirit is asking me to share with you, so, bless the Lord, let's get started!

Prayer

Lord, open my spiritual eyes and ears to see and hear according to Your will. In Jesus' name. Amen.

PART ONE

Do We Really Need Another Book on Prayer?

CHAPTER 1

What's Really Going On
with Prayer, Anyway?

I f you were wondering if another book on prayer is even necessary, I'd agree that is a valid concern. One of the reasons I'm writing this book is because I was beginning to seriously question if believers even still believed in prayer. I mean *"real prayer"*, not the "Now I lay me down to sleep" kind of praying we do on autopilot. Do we actually believe prayer is important? Do we still believe the Scripture that says the effectual, fervent prayers of righteous people have power to bring about miracles? Do we even still believe in miracles, or do we think they were only given by God to set up the early church?

If we do still believe in prayer and miracles—of course, neither are possible by human merit or willpower, but only through Christ— please explain to me why prayer ministry has almost disappeared as a vital ingredient in the overall ministry of many local churches. How is it that we have allowed ourselves to become so busy doing "churchy stuff" that we now ignore or even avoid prayer?

Has prayer become old school? Is prayer viewed as something the old saints used to do back in the day? Every Wednesday night, you'd find them in tiny churches with hard wooden pews, tarrying at the altar on their knees or bowed low on dusty floors. They'd be weeping and calling on the name of Jesus with all their hearts because they knew they needed His help to survive. They believed in the power of prayer and knew how to get a prayer through to God.

But today, here we are, proud as can be in our huge, magnificent edifices, sitting all comfy in row after row of individual, cushioned seats, with our feet casually crossed over thick, matching, wall-to-wall carpeting. Thanks to our cutting-edge technology, some of us don't even bother bringing our Bibles to church anymore. No need to bother lugging those bulky things around. The media department will put the sermon text and Scripture references up on the screen for us, or if we want, we can look them up on our smart phones.

They'll even display the modern choruses we like up there so we can sing along with the worship team. We don't need those old pew songbooks anymore. Besides, younger people don't like singing those old songs. They bore them, so we decided if we want to draw them in, we better keep the music in step with the times.

I'm suspicious that all of our "progress" and modern "improvements" have caused some to think prayer is another one of those things we don't need as much as they did in the past. And now that we've made it through (on Grandma's prayers, I hope you know), the concept of something like the prayer band she was in sounds rather archaic. Oh no, we don't do prayer in church like that nowadays. Even in many of our personal lives, we prefer to reach out on the Web through social media with a prayer post than go to all the trouble to do it face-to-face or call people on the phone. Call me cyber-challenged if you will, but in my opinion, cyber prayer is a pathetic, plastic substitute for real prayer.

Things like prayer bands have been phased out along with ripped-up old King James Version pew Bibles with missing covers and congregational songbooks full of Grandma's favorite hymns. All that dated stuff has been boxed up in a big stack next to the church organ, covered with a dingy sheet of plastic in a dark, dusty storage corner somewhere.

Is it any wonder that many Christians today see prayer as a perplexing puzzle, with too many misunderstood pieces in confusing disarray to be functional? Due to misuse and loss of some of the key pieces, we can no longer put the big picture of prayer's power back into place. And if we can't put it together, how can we use the power of prayer in furthering God's last days' kingdom agenda?

Without seeing the big prayer picture, how can we grasp the importance of promoting prayer in our churches? The Bible says God's people perish because of a lack of knowledge. Could all this confusion on prayer possibly be because churches aren't providing significant teaching about prayer? Without being taught, how can the saints in today's grace-age church know how to get a prayer through to God? Trial and error is very frustrating, not to mention time consuming, especially when you need an answer to prayer right away!

I'm sorry if I am being offensive or stepping on anyone's denominational toes with my nosy questions and critical observations. I apologize, halfheartedly, but I have to ask the questions. Could the answer possibly be that some of us in the body of Christ have lost our passion for prayer? Are we confused and wandering around in circles in a spiritual desert, without direction or confidence, because we're suffering from prayer deficiency? Are we in a prayer drought; all dried up and parched in our personal and corporate prayer ministries?

Still not convinced? Well, if you consider the body of Christ as a whole, how would you evaluate our spiritual condition? I ask that because some Christians are concerned that the church is sliding into a state of serious spiritual imbalance. I also believe there's an imbalance. The imbalance I see is between teachings on the vital importance of believers seeking to live sanctified, holy lives and teachings that Christlikeness is an ongoing and progressive process through the power of the Holy Spirit.

This natural-to-spiritual transformation can only happen by grace through faith, and it takes place in such a supernatural way, it's no wonder a clear understanding on how to best cooperate with the Holy Spirit in the process eludes many. I'm hearing a huge debate going on as to whether we need to believe and do something or just believe and let it happen on its own.

I wholeheartedly believe that any kind of spiritual imbalance in the body of Christ has more to do with what's happening—or better, not happening—with our prayer lives than anything else. I'm not self-righteously standing on the outside of the problem looking in as I point a bony finger of harsh criticism. I'm standing on the inside, right in the thick of it.

My Personal Struggle

I considered myself neither a hyper–grace advocate or a legalist, but I sensed a serious imbalance in my personal walk with Christ. All I knew was that my life kind of just ... sucked, to be perfectly honest with you. It was like the joy of the Lord had seeped right out of me.

I was secretly and repeatedly fighting battles with discouragement and bouts of depression. I was also feeling stuck in a rut because my song-and-drama ministry suddenly came to a dead stop after thirty years. Everywhere I turned, I found closed doors.

I couldn't find a good reason why this was happening to me. I interpreted it as personal rejection by others, which planted seeds of bitterness in my heart. I was frustrated to say the least! Even so, I just kept trying to look "normal," pretending I was okay and nothing was really wrong. However, I wasn't anything close to okay.

My unremarkable prayer life and developing bipolar spirituality left me even more stuck, until my pain finally reached the point of despair. Desperation forced me to come out of denial about my condition and ask the Lord for help. God, in His omniscience and grace, put it in my heart to begin journaling about prayer. When He did, the Spirit quickly began showing me my prayer life was both the cause of *and* the answer to my problem. Hearing from Him was the only way I would find direction for my life.

A serious thirst for prayer stirred in me, but due to my ignorance on the subject, I didn't come close to having any kind of real confidence in prayer. I needed a revelation on the spiritual principles of prayer and how to get a breakthrough. One journal entry read, "I want to pray the kind of prayers that reach God's throne room and don't just stop at my ceiling." I felt deeply in my heart this was the key to experiencing a fresh anointing of His purpose in my life. If I could learn these powerful principles, I could effectively use prayer as a co laborer with God to see that His will was done not only in my life but also in the lives of others.

Jesus promises me in His Word that the Holy Spirit was given to guide me into all truth. His Word also promises me that if I seek Him, I will find Him if I search for Him with all my heart. He hears and answers effectual, fervent prayers, and they accomplish much for the kingdom of God. Based on these promises, I embarked on a quest to carefully search through the Bible for deep insight on prayer. With a committed heart and the Holy Spirit as my guide, I made careful journal notes of everything I learned.

I had a dream a few days after I started my study on prayer. When I awakened, for the life of me, I couldn't remember what the dream was about. All I remembered was that while I was asleep, the word *syllabus* rang in my ears. It kept ringing until I opened my eyes and said, "Syllabus! Syllabus! Syllabus! … Syllabus!" It was like someone was screaming it into my ears to wake me up.

When I woke up and thought about it, I'm embarrassed to admit, I had no idea what the word *syllabus* even meant. I immediately reached for my dictionary and discovered it was defined as "an outline or a summary of the main points of a text, lecture, or course of study."

That's an interesting bit of trivia, I said to myself, *but what does that have to do with anything?* I didn't connect it to what I was studying and journaling on prayer until I began my devotions that morning. As I waited before the Lord, a still small voice of the Spirit told me that what I had begun writing on prayer was to become a type of syllabus. With this one word, He transformed my whole concept from journaling about prayer for personal edification to writing a how-to book on prayer, so I could share with others the truths He was showing me.

The title *School of Prayer* came to me a little later that day while driving to work. In the days that followed, He inspired me to add *Time for a Revolution!* as a subtitle because the type of dramatic change I needed in my ideas about prayer would require nothing short of a revolution, and I was not alone in this.

He was leading me into a new season in my life with a new assignment, and the closed doors of ministry were His work. It required a sabbatical from drama and singing until further notice to ensure my focus remained on this writing assignment until completion.

I was relieved to discover the closed doors were His work, and I loved to write. However, I felt overwhelmed with the idea of laying aside what I knew how to do, to write a book on a subject I knew so little about. I'd worked on a variety of writing projects over the years, but I'd never actually completed a book. He let me know this writing assignment had to be quickly completed, but before I took steps forward, I had to back up and hit the Erase button.

Many bad prayer habits had to be unlearned, and religious, preconceived ideas and misconceptions about prayer and how it worked discarded. Immediately after I embraced the concept of starting with a totally clean slate, the Holy Spirit started revealing truths to me. I listened to His voice and Scripture only, and avoided material from others on the subject of prayer. As He whispered to my spirit, I recorded what I heard.

This book is the documentation of my entry into a spiritual school of prayer with the Holy Spirit as my Teacher in a daily process of expanding me to a deeper level of biblical insight. I'm not even close to a biblical scholar, but I thought I knew a little bit about the Bible after thirty-eight years of studying it. However, what the Holy Spirit is teaching me reveals just how much I don't know, confirming to me that He is using me to write this book. But I'm not in control; He is.

In a fresh, new way, He's putting together a supernatural puzzle by merging new biblical insight with the few bits and pieces of truth I had. The big picture coming into view is much broader and more encompassing than I could have ever imagined. Each day, the Spirit was personally answering the question of whether another book on prayer was needed, and His answer to me was, "Yes. Yes. Yes!"

This is where the revolution part comes in. The Spirit was miraculously revealing sound biblical answers to my questions so that I could finally solve my personal prayer mystery and also radically help others put their own confusing prayer puzzle pieces all together. Discerning the full power of prayer would begin a prayer revolution in the body of Christ beginning with those whose spirits were receptive to truth!

I am in total awe and very excited about all of this. It's always humbling to be used by God, and I'm more thankful than I can possibly express for the awesome privilege of Him using me for this new assignment. Not only am I personally gaining a deeper understanding of prayer, I'm growing in spiritual maturity by leaps and bounds. Best of all, I'm growing so sweetly in my intimacy with my Lord.

I'm thrilled that you took the time to read this first chapter! Perhaps this information seems unremarkable to you. It may read like just more old news. Maybe you're telling yourself, "I've heard it before," and you intend to toss this book aside when you get through these last two paragraphs.

If so, thanks for your time. I sincerely hope you can make use of the blank prayer journal appendixes at the end of this book. I would greatly appreciate it if you would take a moment, right now, to pray for those who will make the decision to continue.

On the other hand, if you're one of those it resonates with, if you also struggle in confusion and frustration with your prayer life, if you have many unanswered questions and need answers, I hope you will keep reading and join me in this refreshing and exciting spiritual learning experience.

Prayer

Holy Spirit, we acknowledge You as the Spirit of Truth. We ask for Your powerful help because we desire to grow together, not just in our demystification and understanding of prayer, but in our daily walk with our Lord. We want to be revolutionized, fully equipped and confident as mighty prayer warriors, knowing we're fully covered by Christ's righteousness. Teach us how to continually offer up fervent, effectual prayers to God in You. Thank You, Father, for Your amazing grace shown to us in Christ. Because of it, we believe that by the end of this book, we will be able to rejoice together in the spirit realm, giving You the glory, honor, and praise in the name of Jesus Christ. Amen.

Welcome to the *School of Prayer—Time for a Revolution!*

Chapter 2

Pssst. What's Going On in Your Prayer Closet?

I don't know a Christian who would not quickly agree with me that spending some time in their prayer closet is a vital element for successful Christian living. When I say "prayer closet," I'm not necessarily talking about a literal closet used for praying. If your closets look anything like mine, well it would take a miracle to even get into one of them.

Most Christians who pray on any regular basis have a special spot in their home where they feel secure. It's a place they can pray in privacy. But the question is, if anyone had a hidden camera and could secretly peek into that place, wherever that is, how often would they find us praying? A look into many of our daily lives might reveal an embarrassing tendency toward habitual praying, ineffective ritualistic praying, or worse—frequent long periods of prayerlessness.

It's natural to lean toward what we know best and to respond to what seems practical to us. Conversely, the natural human tendency is to shy away from or even deny what we don't fully comprehend and to avoid responding to what we think is impractical. Things we don't comprehend automatically fall into the "impractical" category. Those types of things in life are avoided or ignored.

By taking a careful look at the questions I asked earlier, your responses will help us determine if prayer is practical or impractical to you, especially when you're under pressure. Your responses or lack thereof may reveal you are suffering from prayer anemia. Please don't get offended. "Prayer anemia," for lack of a better term, is not just something backslidden Christians suffer from. Even many God-loving, born-again believers suffer from it occasionally. I was one of them.

This spiritual malady results from lacking the practical how-to of effective prayer; the powerful kind of prayer talked about in the book of James.

Therefore confess your sins to each other and pray for each other so that you may be healed. The prayer of a righteous person is powerful and effective.
(James 5:16)

If someone asked you, "Are you a righteous person?" what would be your answer? Many Christians would be very hesitant to respond one way or another without some kind of disclaimer. Few have the confidence to answer that question with assurance because they don't want to sound self-righteous, proud, or arrogant.

Since James qualifies the kind of person it takes to approach God as a "righteous person," those who don't consider themselves that way tend to back-shelve prayer until they have done the things that make them feel righteous. The result of a lack of knowledge and understanding about our state of righteousness being in Christ can cause us to downgrade prayer to an anemic blend of memorizations and imaginings of what we think God might consider the righteous thing to say to Him.

Life's pressures can build up so great that on occasions, we can explode into episodes of something I call "emotional outburst praying." When that happens, all we can do is weep uncontrollably, begging and crying out to God for mercy. The stress-releasing catharsis experienced after this tsunami of tears soothes our soul and makes our emotions feel a little better, but does it really do any spiritual good?

Well, without a doubt, God is merciful. He deeply cares about our tears, but when it comes to prayer, it takes more than a broken heart to get His response. It takes faith and truth—with a fully yielded heart—for a prayer to qualify as being powerful and effective.

When we revert to these ineffective prayer techniques, it's usually because we're in a state of desperation and don't know what else to do.

My people are destroyed from lack of knowledge. (Hosea 4:6)

But our not knowing is no excuse. The Scripture tells us everything we need is provided to us.

His divine power has given us everything we need for a godly life through our knowledge of him who called us by his own glory and goodness. (2 Peter 1:3)

We may mean well, but emotional-outburst praying or impersonal prayer using a religious-sounding recitation or avoidance of prayer altogether out of a fear of doing it wrong are all equally ineffective.

The bottom line is that denying our lack of knowledge of how to pray powerfully and effectively comes at a very, very high price. This is sad when you think of the price Jesus paid with His life to reconcile us to the Father. When He died, the curtain separating the most Holy Place was torn down to give us unhindered access to God's throne of grace. We can take full advantage of that privilege by learning how to pray instantaneously, fervently, constantly, and powerfully in season and out of season!

This freedom of access to God is like possessing a personal invitation to a special endless event with transportation service provided. However, even though we have the invitation in our possession, we don't take the time to actually open it and read, "Round-the-clock limousine service provided by the host." Instead, thinking we don't have a way to get there, we stay at home and miss out on all the good stuff when all we need to do is call for a ride.

Jesus gave us this special invitation and sent us the Holy Spirit as our prayer "ride" to the throne room of God because He knows we cannot get there by ourselves. He is the only way to the Father. It doesn't matter when we call on Him, be it day or night; He is ever ready to take us there. Why not take a minute and tell the Holy Spirit how much you appreciate His ministry in your life?

Prayer

Use your own words.

CHAPTER 3

What's Going On in Church Prayer Ministries?

I don't know if you have noticed, but what I've personally noticed is that something a little strange seems to be going on with church prayer ministries these days. It's like prayer ministry is dwindling away to almost nothing right in front of my eyes. Here are a few of my personal observations at Sunday services that I've attended in different churches of varied denominations in different states over the last few years

Most services opened with music and some kind of liturgy or at least a short pastoral prayer. The bulletin provided as you enter the sanctuary showed where other prayers fit into the Order of Service. The main congregational prayer was handled in various ways.

In some smaller churches, the pastor invited the congregation to come to the front (or altar) for a "do-it-yourself" silent prayer while the musician or choir provided a soft musical background. Some medium to large churches asked the congregation to simply remain at their seats, stand, and bow their heads as the minister in the pulpit offered up general prayers on their behalf. Sometimes a musician or the worship team accompanied the pastor with soft background music during one or all of the prayers.

The more "prayer friendly" churches had a group of specially chosen prayer team members stand up in front of the congregation for a time dedicated to prayer during the worship portion of the service. Those with special prayer needs were invited to come forward to be prayed for by them (and possibly even anointed with oil).

One large church offered a prayer from the pulpit for the congregation or offered an additional opportunity to be prayed for individually by their prayer team immediately following the end of each service (usually minus the oil).

There's a decent chance one of the above models is close to your church's way of handling prayer during services. I find it interesting that the main prayer is normally done early to mid-service, during or after the worship segment and prior to taking the collection, and always before the preaching of the Word.

I'm not sure why, but I assume there's some practical reason for this specific placement. Perhaps it's because most churches offer a salvation prayer or invitation for discipleship right after the preached Word, and they don't want people to be confused about what they're praying for.

What's even more curious is that I notice not all churches do an invitational prayer for salvation after every presentation of the gospel. Some only do it occasionally. I'm not sure why. I wonder if there is an assumption that those present are most likely already believers. I would hope it isn't to avoid the embarrassment to the preacher of no one responding to their invitation. Actually, over the years I've heard sermons in more than a few churches that fell a bit shy of what I'd consider an actual presentation of the gospel, but it's probably better not to go there.

I know one of the purposes of the song worship part of the service is to help the congregation get "in the Spirit" and ready their hearts to receive the preaching of the gospel. Hearing the Word of God preached builds believers up in faith and in truth. When you think about it, if we really believe praying in faith is powerful, having prayer after the delivery of the Word when believers are in the Spirit and most built up in faith and truth would seem to me to be the most productive time to pray, wouldn't it?

I have to ask. Could it be possible that fervent prayer and manifestation of miracles are no longer considered appropriate for regular Sunday services? Are we trending toward thinking these special moves of the Spirit should be done in a different environment—perhaps in a more intimate gathering of believers? Maybe the privacy of our home on our own time is preferable? If that is the case, why?

By the Way ... Where'd the Altars Go?

As I said before, back in the olden days of the church, the saints used to spend a lot of time at the altar at every service, but when the next generation took over and drew up the floor plan for the big, new-and-improved church, the altar seemed to be missing from some of their new floor plans. Perhaps they wanted to maximize space for a nice, big, fancy pulpit area above floor level and make sure there was room enough for a couple of velvet oversized, padded pastor chairs.

Although many don't have organs anymore, some still needed room to accommodate a baby grand piano, or a couple of electric keyboards, lots of guitars, several monitors, and a big drum set or two and conga drums. Don't forget the choir loft and the worship team singers will need standing room up there, and there has to be space enough for the praise dancers and the drama team to be able to move around and do their thing!

Of course the large projection screens will be elevated so that everyone can see, but there still needs to be enough open space left so people can see around all of that without anyone being blocked. After the pulpit area is all situated, the remaining space on the floor plan needs to be allocated to maximize seating for the congregation.

Sometimes the only thing between the congregational seating and the edge of the pulpit area are the steps leading up to it or just enough open space on the floor level for ushers to be able to walk across the front from one side to the other. So some churches use the steps up to the pulpit as an "altar" of sorts, but that seems a little strange to my old-school church altar mentality.

Back in the day, the altar and the pulpit were both considered holy areas with limited access. The altar was a place to bow down, not a transportation zone to be trampling across to get up and down from the pulpit. Some churches considered the pulpit such holy ground that you couldn't even walk across it if you weren't an ordained minister. But I shouldn't be so judgmental; I guess churches are just multitasking and needing to use space more efficiently. I'm probably just too old-fashioned to be talking about the altar topic.

Even so, I wonder if the term *altar* is even part of the average twenty-first-century believer's spiritual vocabulary, because not many churches even talk about the altar anymore. I've yet to see anything close to "altar time" posted in any church bulletin I've seen. It's fairly rare to hear a pastor ask the people to come to the altar, especially in larger churches, (that is if they actually even have an altar), but I've heard some do it.

Tarrying at the altar is not a common practice in most of today's churches. I'm guessing that having two or three services each Sunday morning doesn't leave any time for tarrying. The crowds have to be herded out after the earlier services to make room for the later group coming in. Apparently, the key to success with multiple Sunday services is to maintain a tight schedule or they just won't work.

It has to all be timed just right, you know: thirty minutes is allocated for opening prayer, worship, announcements, and collection; and that leaves the speaker thirty minutes for the sermon and a closing prayer. I can almost hear the defense. "The Bible says everything is to be done decently and in order. So what's the problem of having services well scripted? And just for the record, we welcome the Holy Spirit in our services!"

Perhaps you do, but I wonder, is He being invited with the condition to find the appropriate place in the program, or is He expected to limit His movement in a way that will not disrupt the tight timeline? Otherwise, nothing but confusion would ensue—not to mention a huge traffic jam of first, second, and third service attendees tripping all over each other as they try to come and go!

I guess it's pretty clear that in the new-and-improved kind of church, altars by their very nature may be too difficult to control time wise. Sunday services are now considered by some as a time for teaching and preaching and for enjoying a taste of congregational worship. There's no longer time for unhindered prayer sessions and tarrying at the altar or extended worship sessions carried over by a move of the Spirit during a regular Sunday service. I wonder if those participating in some part of the service ever think to themselves, "I wish I had more freedom. I'm sensing a move of the Spirit, but I'd better stick to the timeline or I may get in trouble!"

Speaking of prayer sessions, tell me something. What's up with weekly prayer meetings at churches? I have a few questions to ask: Does your church still have a weekly prayer meeting for the general congregation? I'm not talking about a quick prayer before or after Bible study. Neither am I talking about a period when the sanctuary is left open and unattended for individuals to come and go for prayer. I mean a scheduled prayer meeting for the whole congregation dedicated to praying *together* as a body. If you have them, how much emphasis (if any) is given to these prayer meetings in Sunday's bulletin or in the special announcements of upcoming week activities?

If you currently attend a church that still offers traditional weekly prayer meetings, tell me when was the last time you attended one? If you haven't gone recently, can I ask why you haven't? If you have recently checked one out, how well attended was it? And if you managed to persevere going to the prayer meetings long enough to be considered a regular attendee, were the meetings vibrant and growing in attendance or was it usually the same small, familiar group of people week after week?

Now tarry a moment (pardon my pun) and do an overview of your church's overall spiritual health. When or if prayer meetings started lowering or increasing in importance and attendance compared to the other scheduled activities of the church, do you think it would make any noticeable spiritual difference in your congregation?

I hope you don't mind me being so personal and nosy, but when was the last time, other than when watching a famous evangelist on Christian TV, that you've personally seen anyone publicly anointed with oil, laid hands on, and prayed for by a pastor or preacher during a Sunday service with the confident expectation of a miracle according to James 5:14?

Wait! I better qualify that question a bit more before you answer. I'm not talking about yearly revival week services or visits by special guest evangelists. I'm talking about regular Sunday services. This kind of hands-on ministry was normative for the early church, but why is the biblical mandate to do it no longer seen as normal?

Do you think many mainline churches today would consider the biblical practice of laying on of hands during a regular Sunday gathering as normal, or would it be seen as a strange and unusual thing to do?

I'm going to go even deeper. I'm curious to know whose "hands on" (pardon the pun) responsibility is the church's prayer ministry where you attend? Do the deacons and elders run it, and who—if anyone—is providing any significant biblical teaching on prayer to the congregation?

I've probably irritated you a bit, haven't I (especially if you are in church leadership)? But please don't toss this book into a corner and call me names! Okay, you can call me names, but keep reading anyway. I'm not some Pharisee wannabe on a spiritual lint-picking expedition or someone being negative about the organized church just to start an argument. I love the church and I'm concerned, very concerned! That is why I'm asking …

- What's up with prayer meetings these days, and how important is prayer ministry in the today's churches?
- Do we still believe in the power of agreement in prayer?
- Do we still even believe in prayer?

- If the church knows we are in the final days of the age of grace, why can't we see that we need to pray like never before?

There is an old movie I grew up with that makes me feel like a little girl when I watch. Whenever I think of this movie, it brings wonderful memories to my mind, and I still, to this day, love to watch it. I'm not going to name the movie. Let's see if you can figure it out on your own.

The characters of the movie were traveling together and had to endure many difficulties and problems as they made their way to their destination. Each of them had a personal handicap or need that caused them to meet each other in the first place, and they each needed a solution. Their weaknesses were manipulated by their antagonist to create problems along the way in an effort to prevent them from reaching their destination. The antagonist tried everything to destroy them, but each trial actually bound them together in unity because they had to help each other to survive. It didn't take them long to discover they were better together than they were struggling alone.

There was a specific scene in that movie that came to mind as I was finishing this chapter. In this scene, this group of needy individuals was traveling along and finally their destination was within sight. It was beautiful and gloriously gleaming atop a hill that seemed oh so close. They became very excited and began to run with all their might.

In their excitement to reach their destination, they didn't realize they needed to be even more careful of the tricks of their enemy. As they ran, they entered a beautiful flowery field. They were breathing very heavily from the run and didn't notice that with each step forward, they were becoming more and more drowsy and tired. It never occurred to them that something as beautiful as a flowery field would need to be traveled through with so much caution and care.

What appeared to be beautiful flowers weren't just regular blossoms. Along with the captivating scent was a substance that heavily drugged the air. With their lungs filled to the max, some could not resist the intoxicating effect, and disappeared from view as they fell into soft, floral yellow pillows into a deep, deep drug-induced sleep.

I think some in the body of Christ are like that group of characters. That gleaming city on the hill is heaven. We are still human, so each of us has a sin handicap of one type or another. The commonality of our sin nature binds us together in hope that when we reach that city, we will experience perfect healing from this malady. Every tear will be wiped from our eyes and every dream will be fulfilled. Seeing the signs around us, we can't help but know we're closer to our destination now than we've ever been. We're so close we can almost see the light of our King's glory.

As we get nearer, we are pressing forward but have underestimated our enemy's clever tactics. He has from the beginning found a way to take the most beautiful blossoms of God's truths, and tweak and distort them by mixing in lies hidden so very subtly that the fragrance of the truth renders the lie nearly undetectable.

We know grace is God's most generous gift to us. How could we be so naive to not expect the Devil to target something as magnificent as grace to try and create confusion and divisions? His scheme is to blend just enough of a lie into the truth that even grace itself could be used to hinder the church's progress. Like the discovery of a beautiful flower field, the church is dancing and running amidst a fragrant flower garden of grace. Teaching and preaching on grace is becoming so prevalent that the air is literally thick with it wherever you turn. But like the unsuspecting group in my favorite movie, many of us are deeply breathing in the teaching, delirious with joy and freedom. We think there is no need to filter any element of the pleasant bouquet because there couldn't possibly be anything about the teaching on grace that could ever hinder our progress.

People are falling totally intoxicated into the pillow softness of grace, into a deep, deep sleep. They are sleeping soundly on our left and on our right, oblivious to the danger. If you are one of the sleepers, what I am saying right now may greatly offend you. To you, my observations may even sound like the rantings of a legalist who is against teaching grace. But that is far, far from the truth.

The grace of God is glorious and magnificent! To me, true grace is not a teaching. Grace is a person, and His name is Jesus Christ, who is the center of my life! He sacrificed Himself so that I could be reconciled to His Father through faith in Him. Jesus is the way of grace, the truth of grace, and the life of grace.

If I've irritated you, try to consider what I'm saying before you reject it. Take a deep, clear, cleansing breath and keep reading, because I have an important message from the Lord of grace.

God wants us to remember the antagonist of the church ever lives to steal, kill, and destroy. In this human drama we call life, the Devil would love to rewrite the script with an ending other than him being tossed into the lake of fire—but he can't. All he can do is try to take as many with him as possible. Since the Devil can't stop grace or prevent Christians from ultimately reaching our gleaming heavenly city, he set his agenda to try every trick he can to slow us down. He hopes to take advantage of the element of surprise by using the most pleasant and lovely things as stumbling blocks; things we would never expect him to use.

One of his targets is the beautiful teaching on the grace of God; distorting it just enough so his manipulation of the truth is hidden. The distortion is presented in a way that won't be easily detected while he accomplishes his objective of hindering the progress of the church. The end result in these later years of the grace age is that a segment of the body of Christ has bought into his trick and thinks that because of grace,

- prayer bands and tarrying at the altar are examples of human effort (works) to try and reach God;
- poor attendance at prayer meetings shows they aren't desired or needed by the congregation;
- praying, anointing, and laying hands on people during church services is unnecessary, and besides that, it's too showy and excessive; and

- prayers of repentance imply the sin debt has not been paid in full by Christ.

My take is that they consider activities like these that put so much focus on prayer as falling into the category of "works." In their understanding of grace, these are actually counterproductive. Some even seem to be teaching that grace eliminates the need for believers to offer prayers of repentance. Repentance implies an awareness of sin, and since Christ paid for our sin in full, according to them, awareness of sin is not a good thing.

An awareness of sin only causes people to sin more not sin less. But teachings that say there is no need to be concerned about sin and repentance don't line up well with the final message of the Spirit to the seven churches in Revelation 2 and 3.

To be honest with you, when I first started listening to some of the preaching on grace, it made me feel really good about myself! It seemed to say to me that I shouldn't ever think about my shortcomings or repenting of sin. Regardless of the sin in my life, because I am in Christ, I already have everything I need so I should only occupy my mind with walking and talking like all is well. If I do this continually and just ignore sin, it will eventually go away on its own. In the meantime, I can expect every need I claim in Christ's name to materialize. All this is because of grace.

Now doesn't that sound just great? Scripture is provided to support all of this. I have noticed heavy emphasis on the Word, but the focus seems to be almost entirely on Scriptures about grace. I agree that understanding what God's Word has to say to us about grace is very important, but what about the rest of God's truths? God's grace toward us is based on His love. But the Bible also says God's love causes Him to discipline and rebuke us as His children in our struggle against sin.

**My son, do not despise the Lord's discipline,
and do not resent his rebuke,**

> **because the Lord disciplines those he loves,**
>   **as a father the son he delights in.**
> **(Proverbs 3:11–12)**

I can almost hear you say, "Okay, but that verse is from the Old Testament. That's how God dealt with people's sin under the old covenant. God deals with us differently now because we are not under old covenant of law, but we are under the new covenant of grace through Christ! Yes, thank God for the new covenant of grace. Salvation is by grace through faith alone and not of ourselves. But please tell me why He repeats these verses in the New Testament applying them to those who have already received Christ?

> **In your struggle against sin, you have not yet resisted to the point of shedding your blood. And have you completely forgotten this word of encouragement that addresses you as a father addresses his son? It says,**
> **"My son, do not make light of the Lord's discipline, and do no lose heart when he rebukes you, because the Lord disciplines those he loves, and he chastens everyone he accept as a son."**
> **(Hebrews 12:4–6)**

Also, notice these verses calling the church to repentance in the very last book of the Bible:

> **Those whom I love I rebuke and discipline. So be earnest, and repent. Here I am! I stand at the door and knock. If anyone hears my voice and opens the door, I will come in and eat with that person, and they with me.**
> **(Revelation 3:19–20)**

Overcoming and experiencing victory in our struggle against sin begins with being truthful with ourselves and with God in prayer! When there is no admission (consciousness) of sin, there will be no sense of need for prayers of confession or repentance. That really bothers me because it just doesn't line up with the Word.

> **If we claim to be without sin, we deceive ourselves and the truth is not in us. If we confess our sins, he is faithful and just and will forgive us our sins and purify us from all unrighteousness. If we claim we have not sinned, we make him out to be a liar and his word is not in us.**
> **(1 John 1:8–10)**

There are many high-powered teachers and preachers with huge followings teaching almost entirely on grace these days. My complaint is not that they are emphasizing grace; grace should be emphasized in every presentation of the gospel. My complaint is that too many Christians allow themselves to become overly dependent on their favorite teachers and preachers as their primary source of spiritual nourishment. An addiction to a certain "flavor" of truth can grow to such an extreme that followers end up swallowing whole whatever they are spoon-fed without even bothering to chew it up.

Too few Christians are going directly to the source of truth on a daily basis to seek the Holy Spirit in prayer, studying and meditating on the Word of God and asking Him to feed them a well-balanced spiritual meal and keep them full. Experience has taught me that if I expose myself to any particular teaching that is even marginally unbalanced, when I spend time alone praying and studying the Bible in the Spirit relative to that teaching, He always brings me discernment. His full revelation of the whole truth on any subject always returns me to sound scriptural balance.

That is why I sift every presentation of truth I receive from each and every source through the filter of God's Word and presence. The

Holy Spirit of truth was sent by Christ to be our primary teacher. He is the best source for truth and will keep the cookies on a low-enough shelf that all His children can access them regardless of their level of spiritual maturity.

You may disagree with my perceptions on how grace is being taught by some, but that's okay. To be quite honest, I didn't start this chapter on prayer ministry in the church with the intention of writing about grace. It just started to flow that direction. In my first draft, I had written a much longer and stronger section on grace than what you are reading now. I deleted a lot during an early edit. I was concerned that some of my comments, if taken the wrong way, would prove counterproductive to my goal. I decided to save those observations for a book entirely on the subject of grace, which I intend to write at a later date.

So, if this edited portion on grace ticks you off, believe me, you definitely wouldn't have appreciated what was cut. I left this much in because I sensed God could still use this toned-down section on grace as a gentler wake-up call than what was originally here. Every day more and more Christians are jumping on the grace boat, but not very many are willing to rock the boat by honestly talking about the subject. It is difficult to try and paddle uphill, but I had to speak up because the teaching was becoming really popular with the masses.

As I looked around, I saw too many Christians comfortably asleep on the boat, and I believed God wanted to wake us up to prepare us for an approaching storm. If we hear His still small voice, awaken from grace sleepiness, and turn toward Him in prayer, we will begin to see our true condition through His eyes. But He has given us free will, and that means we have a choice whether we will respond to His call or whether we will not. Only when we respond and develop ears willing to hear will we discern what the Spirit is saying to the church in this late hour.

He's coming soon. I know the Word says only God knows the actual day and hour of Christ's return, but I doubt that even the harshest skeptics of date setting would disagree that the signs of the times we live in indicate the Lord's coming is very, very soon. The very times themselves are screaming at us, "Wake up, you people! Hello! Hello! We're trying to show you it's the last of the last days!"

It doesn't take much spiritual discernment to recognize that much of the grace-age church is snoozing away; we're fast asleep at a time we need to be watching and fervently praying in power! We need to wake up from our gracious slumber and seek the face of God like never before so we can get end-time instructions from Him!

Now just in case you are questioning if this book is teaching prayer as a work of human effort, let me say it clearly: I am not presenting prayer as a human work required by God to try and earn His favor and/or approval. All righteousness, favor, and approval come by grace through faith in Christ alone. It can never be earned by any work. Besides that, true prayer—the only kind that gets through to God—is not a work of the flesh. Prayer is a spiritual interaction with God. It is a privilege of access to God's throne only to those who are in Christ.

I believe that when the Bible tells us to "pray without ceasing," it is saying the same thing as when it says we are to spiritually "abide in Christ." Praying without ceasing is living in constant, intimate communion with Him. When we abide in Christ, we trust His finished work, and by faith we can experience the fullness and power of all He accomplished for us!

If you are still a skeptic, extend me a wee little bit more grace by giving me the benefit of the doubt. In other words, by all means, try to continue reading with an open mind.

Prayer

Take a moment to offer up a prayer asking God to use this book for His glory.

PART TWO

Understanding Prayer

CHAPTER 4

Prayer Is a Mystery!

rayer is an interaction between natural human beings existing in the natural realm *in time* with almighty God who exists in the supernatural realm of the Spirit *in eternity*. If that relationship itself isn't a great mystery, I don't know what is! Our relationship with God, who is Spirit, is not a natural relationship, it's a supernatural one, and that isn't an easy concept to grasp. As a matter of fact, it's a concept that the natural human mind can never grasp. It can only be spiritually discerned.

The word *prayer* has become so common in our language and so basic to Christianity that I think many of us simply take its meaning for granted. In Old English, "I pray thee" and "I ask thee" have the same meaning and were often used interchangeably. If we, today, understand "to pray" as just meaning, "to ask," that would greatly affect our understanding of what prayer is and its purpose.

Jesus apparently spent a significant amount of His time on earth praying to the Father. He prayed instinctively, constantly, and vigorously. In the garden prior to His arrest, He prayed with such intensity that He sweat drops of blood. Knowing what we know about His relationship with His Father and all the authority and power He had been given on earth, it would be hard for me to imagine Him spending all that time asking His Father for things. Prayer must be more than just asking—much, much more!

Although prayer was instinctive to Jesus, it's not instinctive to us; it is a learned behavior. The disciples realized there was something very different and powerful about Christ's praying. They wanted to learn what it was so they could pray like He did, so they asked Jesus, "Teach us to pray." He gave them a sample prayer known to us as The Lord's Prayer. We'll look at that more closely a little later.

Some assume that knowing how to pray comes as naturally as breathing. To them, it doesn't require all that much forethought; it's something you just do. They might even say they already know all they need to know about prayer, and a book like this may seem trivial or even unnecessary to them. To people of this mind-set, the thought of actually asking Jesus to teach them to pray like the disciples did would never come to mind.

To be honest, prayer wasn't something I thought that much about either. I admit, I didn't have a lot of confidence or expectation when it came to my prayers being answered, but I thought that was just the way it was with most Christians. I saw prayer as a special spiritual gift some people had, and the rest of us just did the best we knew how or asked the gifted few to pray for us.

I didn't know how much I needed to learn on the subject until the Spirit gave me this writing assignment. After the Spirit started opening my heart to understanding, it didn't take me long to realize how misinformed I was on prayer. He began showing me what a great mystery prayer actually is!

In him and through faith in him we may approach God with freedom and confidence. (Ephesians 3:12)

It is a mystery that such boldness and access to the Father has been made available through Christ. The plan for this access was hidden for ages in God, but now the church is making God's manifold wisdom known to the rulers and authorities in heavenly places. What had been kept secret now has been revealed. The mystery is that Christ Jesus was given as the Savior of not just Jews, but of the whole world. The riches of this mystery is Christ in us and our oneness with Him. This is our hope of glory that is being prepared for us. This glory is magnificently beyond anything we can imagine, and it will not be fully revealed until His second coming.

> **However, as it is written:**
> **"No eye has seen, no ear has heard, no mind**
> **has conceived what God has prepared for**
> **those who love him"—but God has revealed**
> **it to us by his Spirit.**
> **The Spirit searches all things, even the deep**
> **things of God.**
> **(1 Corinthians 2:9–10)**

God reveals mysteries by the Spirit to those who love Him and desire His presence and His will in their lives. He reveals Himself to those who meditate on His Word and spend time sitting at His feet in prayer. Christ is the mystery of God being revealed to seekers.

> **"Ask and it will be given to you; seek and you**
> **will find; knock and the door will be opened to**
> **you. For everyone who asks receives; and the one**
> **who seeks finds; and to the one who knocks, the**
> **door will be opened.**
> **(Matthew 7:7–8)**

I don't think Jesus is talking about just material things. He knows what we need before we ask. I think He is talking about things of the Spirit. He said that seeking the kingdom and His righteousness should be first; everything else we need will be added.

> **If you then, though you are evil, know how to**
> **give good gifts to your children, how much more**

> **will your Father in heaven give the Holy Spirit to**
> **those who ask him!**
> **(Luke 11:13)**

In Mark 4:11, Jesus told His disciples the secrets of the kingdom of God are only given to and known by His followers. I believe prayer is one of the secrets of the kingdom of God, and it's a great power that needs to be unleashed in the body of Christ in these last days. Prayer is a mystery that is being ignored by many, and greatly underestimated and misunderstood by others because the mystery of prayer is only revealed to those with ears to hear. *That is why we need another book on prayer!*

But before we go much further in trying to unravel this mystery called prayer, I want to make sure we're beginning on the same page. I feel the need to ask the Spirit to help us clear up a few things.

Prayer

Lord, we seek You with our whole hearts. We admit our understand may be much too shallow and we may be missing the real purpose prayer has been given to us. Please reveal to us what prayer is and what prayer isn't. Transform our concept of prayer and renew our minds in truth. In Jesus' name we pray. Amen.

So in the next chapter, let's consider first what prayer *isn't*.

CHAPTER 5

What Prayer Isn't

Amiss

A miss prayer is asking with wrong motives. It is asking God to give us a bunch of selfish stuff to satisfy our carnal nature. I like the way James 4:3 is translated in KJV: "Ye ask, and receive not, because ye ask amiss, that you may consume it on your lusts."

James was writing to correct carnally minded people. The chapter talks about infighting in the church as they constantly battled one another for very selfish reasons. Instead of walking in the Spirit in unity, they were walking in the flesh in division. Instead of seeking first the kingdom of God and His righteousness, then submitting their needs to Him in prayer, the lust for worldly things controlled them.

Their carnality lured them into conformity with the worldly attitude that "God helps those who help themselves," so it also came "natural" to their old man to viciously and aggressively attack each other in a greedy effort to help themselves to all they wanted. He told them their praying was amiss, but I think this category of prayer can be broadened to include any selfish or willful prayer offered intentionally or even ignorantly outside of God's revealed will.

Self-willed prayers are never prayed in the Spirit but are prayed in the flesh and motivated by selfish carnal desires. God doesn't respond to those kinds of prayers. Selfish, willful prayers go unanswered because they are unspiritual. They don't rise any higher than the ceiling. If I called for a show of hands of those who have wasted time praying amiss kinds of prayers, I'd be the first to raise both my hands.

Habitual Religious Prayers

Prayer Isn't a Religious Habit

Habitual prayers as a routine are usually done in powerless autopilot. Given the benefit of doubt, I think the formality of these prayers is very sincere for the most part. I believe some think formality is more honoring to God, and being too comfortable or relaxed in prayer is just flat-out irreverent and unholy. So they created a formal prayer language of sorts just in case they got overly excited or carried away and accidentally blew it.

Formality works very well with memorization and establishment of routines. Now don't misunderstand me, having a daily prayer routine is a very good thing if we can keep it fresh, but I wonder how many of our prayer routines go a bit like this.

Every morning upon awaking, we punch an invisible time clock and our routine begins:

A) Checking in. Our a.m. prayer is repeated: "Lord, give me strength to face this day ..."

B) All meals elicit the "Thank you for this food ..." prayer before taking a single bite.

C) Checking out. Finally, our p.m. prayer at the end of the day finishes it off. Just before falling asleep we say a drowsy, "Now I lay me down to sleep ..."

Then off to sleep we go, feeling pretty good about ourselves. We can sleep soundly knowing we satisfactorily checked off the "prayers done" box on our daily to-do list. As *good* Christians, we once again completed our daily prayer religious routine! Just in case I didn't quite get the point across, let me elucidate a bit more with this fictitious example.

Let's say a nice, disciplined girl named Sue who loved routines (mostly because they made her feel more in control) had a sister named May. She loved her sister a lot but didn't get to see her very often because May lived far out of town. So Sue, being the good and considerate sister that she was, established a routine of calling May every morning.

It was time for Sue's 8:00 a.m. call to her sister, but she was so busy organizing her schedule for the day and trying to remember each thing she had to put on her to-do list that she totally lost track of time (heaven forbid!). When she finally did look up at the clock, she began feeling anxious and stressed seeing it was already 9 a.m., and she hadn't yet made her routine sisterly call!

Where had all the time gone? This meant she would only have fifteen minutes before she had to leave for her first appointment. She considered skipping the call altogether, not because she didn't care about her sister or enjoy their daily chats, but there just wasn't enough time left to discuss anything in detail. Their calls usually lasted about an hour. Knowing her sister would be expecting her call, she picked up her cell phone and hit the 'May" Auto-dial button. She was hoping it would go to voice mail, but May answered with an extra cheery, "Hellooooo." Sue was a bit curious why her sister sounded so especially happy this morning, but looking again at the clock, she decided to ignore it and skip right to the quick preliminaries.

"Morning, sis! How's your morning going so far?" she said energetically, trying to mimic May's cheery tone. When her sister's response to her matter-of-fact question began to drag on a little too long, Sue changed her tone of voice to a more formal one and cut in with, "Sounds good. What are your plans for today?" Instead of allowing May to finish another lengthy response, she again interrupted midstream and began babbling on about her own busy plans for the day and other small talk, flowing in one continuous sentence.

May made attempts to get back into the flow of the conversation, but Sue wasn't paying much attention to her sister's comments. She was thinking ahead to what she had to do next after the call ended, and she wasn't even listening. She was constantly glancing at the clock. Besides, she knew this conversation was most likely going to be pretty much the same as all the others, so listening wasn't all that crucial. At least it wasn't crucial to her.

Now it was 9:14 with only one minute to wrap things up with her sister. Sue was so busy trying to figure out a polite way to end the conversation, she didn't hear or respond to May's question, "Hey, sis, when can you come this way for a visit?" Sue talked right over May as she attempted to wrap up the conversation. May, after a few seconds with no response to her question, interrupted with a loud, "Hello. Hello, Sue, can you hear me? Well, when can you?"

Shocked, Sue apologetically responded, "Oh, sorry, May. When can I what? Did I miss something you said? We must've temporarily lost our connection. Forgive me. Oh boy, I just noticed I'm running late. It's nine fifteen and I have an appointment I have to get to, but I promise I'll try to call you earlier tomorrow, okay?"

"Whatever," her sister answered, a bit irritated. Their call ended with the usually exchange of "Love you, bye," and Sue quickly hit the End Call button. *Mission accomplished,* she thought to herself with satisfaction as she tucked her phone neatly back into its place in her purse.

Mission accomplished? Really, Sue? She may have felt she accomplished something by completing her daily routine of checking in with her sister, but did she?

Did the conversation have the slightest chance of significance with Sue so distracted with constant clock watching?

Did May get anything out of the formality of Sue's disconnected small talk?

Did May feel even slightly valued by Sue's call?

Did Sue get anything out of the conversation herself considering she was too preoccupied to listen to or care about anything her sister said?

Sue may have made her daily call to May, but did she connect with her? My answer to each question is, I don't think so. Sue's morning call would have accomplished as much if May hadn't answered, and she'd left her a voice mail message containing the same information. Even though May picked up the call and tried her best to draw Sue into a meaningful conversation, she actually experienced a "call failed" because Sue wasn't the least bit in listening mode.

There was a call, but there definitely was no connection. In our habitual religious prayers, we may dial God up on the "Our Father which art in heaven" line, but if we go right into babbling without allowing time for Him to acknowledge and respond, how can we be sure our call got through and we've connected with Him?

The connecting part of prayer is the key to knowing our prayer is being heard. Prayer isn't just regurgitating a lot of high-sounding religious words at God. If we are in such a rush that we consider the connecting part of prayer to be too time consuming, we'll go directly to "auto-dial" and immediately begin babbling away on a dead line. We haven't connected to God. We're only talking to ourselves, whether we realize it or not.

> **And when you pray, do not keep on babbling like pagans, for they think they will be heard because of their many words. (Matthew 6:7)**

Prayer Isn't Religious Ritual

Prayer isn't a religious ritual aimed at impressing God. Pagans take a hunk of wood, a piece of metal or stone, and form themselves gods.

Then they bow down in worship and present empty prayers to them. Praying to the only living God of the entire universe is as different from that as north is from south.

Ritual prayers tend to be very wordy and layered with formality. Those who lean this way love to pray them out loud, especially around others. They often seem to start with something like an "Oh thou most gracious Father of the universe" type of beginning. Sometimes they use King James English all the way through as if that was "God speak" or His personal prayer language preference. After their enthusiastic "Amen!", hearers say, "Oh, how beautifully you pray! Your prayer gave me chills!"

It sounds so doggone pretty and pleasant to their ears that they can't help but respond with admiration for how articulate and confident they sound in prayer. They are asked to pray so often; they become well practiced at it and may even secretly think praying like this is their gift to the body of Christ.

Just as my fictitious example was one of a useless routine call, so are rehearsed, habitual, religious prayers. They are done amiss and accomplish nothing. I'll even go so far as to say they don't value God; they actually devalue Him. Our approach to God must never be mechanical. It must always be worshipful. In John 4:23–24, Jesus told the woman at the well true worship must be in the Spirit and in truth. He said the Father was seeking these kind of worshippers.

David knew a lot about the right attitude of worship. He was a man after God's own heart.

Enter his gates with thanksgiving and his courts with praise; give thanks to him and praise his name.
(Psalm 100:4)

When prayer gets reduced to ritual, it is unknowingly transformed from a live worshipful interaction with God into a burdensome religious action considered as necessary to be a "good"

Christian. It becomes the right thing or expected thing to do at the appropriate time. *You have to* do it at church gatherings of any type. *You have to* do it when you're in a fix. But God never intended prayer to be a 911 God call—something *you have to* keep quick and handy in case of an emergency.

Religious formality praying done habitually out of obligation whether in emergency or not tends to be prepackaged, powerless, and ineffectual no matter how many impressive words are spoken. Others might be impressed, but God isn't. I'm ashamed to say I have been guilty on occasion of offering up these flowery, scripted prayers. What's even worse, in most cases they were only a carnal facade of spiritual correctness.

Any time we're striving to offer a prayer that sounds spiritual to others, it's not even close to being a genuine, heartfelt truly spiritual prayer. It's not in the Spirit, in truth, or in faith. It's merely religious babble. We are not praying to God; we're praying at Him because actually we're really only praying to hear ourselves and to be heard by others because we like the sound of our own voices.

> **The Lord says,**
> "**These people come near to me with their mouth and honor me with their lips, but their hearts are far from me. Their worship of me is based on merely human rules they have been taught.**" (Isaiah 29:13)

Prayer babble is an example of this verse. It is ingenuous and has zero confidence behind it. It intrinsically underestimates the potentially dynamic power biblically based prayers have. It requires no faith to recite a religious formal prayer. It's a prayer so burdened with doubt, it can't possibly get any results and has no chance of resulting in an actual miracle. Jesus told His disciples over and over to pray in faith and not have doubt in their hearts.

Faith and doubt aren't meant to blend together. They are immiscible. In the end, they will always separate. Faith rises heavenward, expecting change without seeing, while doubt sinks to the pits because it has to see or it will never expect change. When we have a doubting heart, we can barely muster up enough shallow hope to imagine just surviving our difficulties.

The Word tells us to pray in faith and in the Spirit. This is the only way we can connect or get a prayer through to God. If we think we can go blasting through the gates into His presence with religious formality, we are mistaken. We only end up with something close to the automated message we get from a misdial: "This number is not in service. If you have reached this number in error, please dial again."

If we want to get through, to enter God's presence, we have to redial with worship in the Spirit. Only then does the spiritual connection happen and a real conversation with Him begin. We'll talk more about this a little later on.

Prayerlessness

This category doesn't mean a total absence of prayer, but it does apply to prayer lives that tend to run hot and cold or only occur on a hit-or-miss basis based on circumstances. A hot-and-cold, hit-or-miss attitude toward prayer is guaranteed if prayer is seen as a time-consuming religious chore or duty that has to be forced into an already over-busy schedule. If prayer only happens on a "need to" frequency, it only takes the slightest external impetus to create such a distraction that the whole prayer process can be shipwrecked midstream.

Should it be any surprise how these distractions tend to conveniently and suspiciously crop up right when you decide to pray? Just as you get into prayer mode, the phone rings or someone loudly calls your name from another room or there's a persistent knock at the front door. Once the devilish distraction has succeeded in diverting your attention away from prayer, even the most well-intentioned, scheduled "need to" prayer gets postponed because now there's not enough time for it.

Then there is that irritating tendency of imagination distractions. Sometimes the most unspiritual, carnal thoughts pop into your head while trying to pray. "Yipes! I hope God didn't see that!" It can be so irritating or guilt producing that you just give up! You reason that you are just too stressed out or distracted to pray right now.

But most frustrating of all, are those awful sleep attacks that ambush during your attempts at early morning or late evening prayer times. There you are lying flat on your back in bed or kneeling against it with your tired body nicely settled in an oh-so-relaxed position. You're ready for your quiet time with God. Of course your eyelids are closed so you can focus on praying and not be distracted by your surroundings.

You barely get started in the prayer preliminaries: "Oh, dear, all-powerful Lord of the universe, I give You praise ...zzzzzzzzz." Right in the middle of your memorized introductory sentence, before you can even get going good, a sense of extreme tiredness drops like an avalanche. Before you can catch yourself, down you go, fast asleep (or back to sleep).

Cup-Half-Empty Prayers

There is a subgroup within the hit-or-miss group that I call the cup-half-empty prayers. They bring to mind a silly saying my sibs and I had when I was a young girl. We'd see a person with a very sour face, then look at each other, giggle, and whisper, "They look like someone promised them something, and they didn't get it."

I'm not sure why we thought that saying was so cute and funny. I've had enough personal hardships and painful experiences in life to know there's nothing at all comical about feeling so disappointed that it shows on your face. Experiencing disappointment over and over can cause a loss of hope. Sour-faced people are hopeless people.

They can't help but see their cup perpetually half empty, never half full.

Hopelessness left unrestrained brings about a bitterness of soul that eventually sours the attitude toward every relationship. It develops into a mind-set that it's better not to ask someone for something than it is to ask and be denied and disappointed once again. A hope-deprived attitude will sour our relationship with God, especially if there's a history of what we see as too many unanswered prayers.

> **Hope deferred makes the heart sick, but a longing fulfilled is a tree of life.**
> **(Proverbs 13:12)**

Hope and faith must be alive and well in our prayer life. For any prayer to be heard by God, it has to be prayed in faith. It takes hope to expect Him to answer prayers.

> **And without faith it is impossible to please God, because anyone who comes to him must believe that he exists and that he rewards those who earnestly seek him.**
> **(Hebrews 11:6)**

Sometimes we foolishly attempt to sidestep the faith requirement for prayer. When we don't get the response we wanted, instead of realigning our will to synchronize with God's will, we try to reason out unanswered prayer by blanketing our lack of faith with a thick layer of human logic. The inner dialogue can sound something like this:

"God is sovereign. The Bible says He is omniscient, omnipresent, and omnipotent, doesn't it? Since God already knows everything— He even knows my thoughts before I think them—won't He automatically give me whatever He wants me to have that lines up with His will for my life? And if He only gives me what's in His will for my life, what's the point of me praying about things I don't know His will about? After all, God is sovereign, and He'll do whatever He pleases in my life, anyway.

"Besides, I already have a long list of unanswered prayers, and I don't want to add to it. Evidently, my long list says I've already prayed and asked for too many things in the past that just weren't according to His will."

This almost sounds logical and even reasonable, doesn't it? That is why the Word tells us not to lean on our own understanding. This kind of carnal reasoning eliminates any need for real faith by trying to use a "God is sovereign" argument. It also flies in the face of the biblical requirement found in 1 Thessalonians 5:17 to pray continually. We are told in Philippians 4:6 to pray about every situation in our lives.

You see, embracing a "God does what He good and well pleases" human-based logic actually discourages prayer. A prayer-deprived Christian soon turns into a hope-deprived, heartsick Christian with a sour disposition that brings no glory or honor to God. Not only is it a truly sad thing to behold, it makes drawing people to Christ nearly impossible.

It's the hope and joy flowing from us that draws people to the light of Christ in us. How can a Christian who looks depressed and disappointed all the time draw anyone to Him? Who in their right mind would desire what they appear to have for themselves?

These are only a few examples of what prayer isn't. I could go on and on, but I think these get the idea across. All misconceptions about prayer are not just unfortunate; they're spiritually counterproductive and can be devastating.

Amiss Prayers. Thinking prayer is a means of submitting our selfish wish list to God as if He were a "genie in a bottle" waiting to fulfill our every command.

Habitual Religious Prayers. Ritualistically offered spiritless prayer in an effort to superficially "check in" with God at our convenience.

Cup-Half-Empty Prayers. Prayer without faith, hope, or expectation.

Prayerlessness. Prayer on a hot-and-cold, hit-or-miss basis.

They're all examples of **what prayer isn't.**

Before we continue, there's something I think I need to say just in case you think I sound somewhat self-righteous and overcritical in the "What Prayer Isn't" chapter. Okay, here goes:

I am *not* writing on the subject of prayer to imply that I think I have all the answers. I don't! As I said at the beginning, I'm *not* writing this book because I thought it was a good idea. It wasn't even my idea. Besides, I'm no one special or noteworthy in Christian circles. I'm *not* writing under the pretense of being a self-proclaimed spiritual know-it-all. I don't have a biblical degree or any of the things the world would say qualifies me to write this book or any kind of book. You may not even consider me that good of a writer— but that's okay. I'm not writing to try and impress you with my literary skills.

I *am* writing because I was told to write, and as a regular garden-variety believer, I needed answers to my personal questions about prayer. I *am* writing because I have too often prayed amiss or allowed myself to fall into religious prayer formality, half-empty-cup praying, or worse—prayerlessness. I am ashamed to admit there have been many, many times I have yielded to shallow daydreaming or flat-out fell into a deep sleep right in the beginning of a prayer. I have experienced disappointment more than once because of unanswered prayer, and I know what it's like to feel very heartsick because of deferred hope.

If these aren't proof enough of my cluelessness about prayer, I also know what it's like to avoid praying altogether because I was afraid to even dare to hope.

I *am* writing because I'm in the battle of my life to hold on to truth, hope, and faith, and because I believe I am not in this battle alone. I eventually discovered this battle is what it means to be a

Christian. I'm not talking about a battle to comprehend spiritual truth just for personal edification. I'm talking about the spiritual warfare for God's truth against the lies of the Devil that's been going on since the time of Adam in the Garden of Eden.

A war over men's souls has been raging for thousands of years. Although Jesus Christ won the battle for us on Cavalry when He cried out, "It is finished," the delivery of the truth about what His life, death, and resurrection accomplished for us is where we come in. This is the truth we are battling to deliver to the world; the truth that can set men free.

You may ask, "Okay, but what does this battle have to do with you writing this book entitled, *School of Prayer—Time for a Revolution!*?

Well, I'm glad you asked! The answer is because prayer is an important and powerful spiritual weapon given to us by God to use in this battle. When you think of the word *school*, you think of learning, and it is only through learning about and understanding prayer that we can maximize our spiritual connection with our Commander in Chief, keeping it vibrant enough to receive clear battle instructions from Him.

I also believe He wants us to learn that prayer is a more spiritually powerful weapon in this battle than we have previously realized, and it must be intimately understood to be effectively used. It isn't simply a weapon to use in defending territory. It's even more powerful as an offensive weapon to use in taking territory for God. Knowing this can make us most effective for the Lord as His warriors of light in this end-time battle against the kingdom of darkness.

That is why I'm writing this! Whew! I really needed to get that off my chest! Thanks for letting me do that.

Prayer

Now, it's your turn. I don't have much doubt that at least one of the prayer inadequacies registered with you. Why not stop and take a moment to offer a prayer in the Spirit, confessing the area(s) where you saw yourself. Ask the Lord to set you free and lead you into the right way to pray.

Now, let's move forward and take a look at the positive side of the prayer equation and see what prayer is.

CHAPTER 6

What Prayer Is

Prayer Is Powerful!

Therefore confess your sins to each other and pray for each other so that you may be healed. The prayer of a righteous person is powerful and effective.
(James 5:16)

The kingdoms of this world are all struggling for power. Countries will invest large percentages of their resources to get the edge over other countries in technology, economy, and military prowess. There is no limit to what some will do in their striving to become a world leader, driven by a lust to dominate and impose their will over other lesser countries.

There is a well-known saying that "all power tends to corrupt, and absolute power corrupts absolutely." History is littered with corrupt leaders whose acts of brutality proved the truth of this statement. The lust for power has too often been the impetus for going to war, and this has not changed much since the beginning of time. It seems to be innate in sinful human nature to yearn for control and dominance over others.

When reduced down to the basic organization of family government, this battle for power and the corrupting influence of its abuse has resulted in the failure of many families. Whenever two individuals demand control and neither is willing to yield, emotional wars wreak havoc. Today's families are burdened with a smorgasbord of dysfunctions that drive many marriages to divorce, but it would be no surprise to discover that "unmet appetite for power" was near the top of the menu.

Natural man only understands natural power. Humans are darkened in their understanding of God's omnipotence because their hearts are hardened by sin's power over them. Unforgiven sin is what alienates men from their all-powerful Creator. It blinds them and prevents them from acknowledging Him as sustainer of all, whether visible or invisible. He is the great and awesome God, and His powerful Word holds all things together! True power is in His hands, and He gives power to whomever He chooses, but unlike man, God's power is not limited to the natural. God's power is supernatural!

When Jesus left this earth, He delegated His power and authority to His followers. He said that they would do greater things than He had done on the earth because He had to return to His Father's throne. He told His disciples to wait for the Holy Spirit to come upon them so they could receive the power they needed to be His witnesses.

On the day of Pentecost, the Holy Spirit was poured out on them, and the disciples displayed powerful signs and wonders as they preached the gospel. Peter was exercising this power in prayer when he raised a woman from the dead.

> **Peter sent them all out of the room; then he got down on his knees and prayed. Turning toward the dead woman, he said "Tabitha get up." She opened her eyes, and seeing Peter she sat up. (Acts 9:40).**

We love to read about the miracles in the New Testament, but the power of prayer did not expire with Peter and the early church. Power is still available to today's church as we obey the Great Commission. By faith, we too can walk in signs and wonders manifesting His power to benefit His kingdom. The indwelling Holy Spirit wants to give this kind of power to the end-time church to enable the expansion of His spiritual kingdom in the earth in preparation of Christ's return to establish His physical kingdom and rule.

He promised that if we have faith as small as a mustard seed, whatever we ask for in prayer we will receive. When prayers are answered, the Father is glorified in the Son. Prayer is powerful!

Prayer Is Spiritual

God is Spirit, and He gave us the new birth so that our spirits can spiritually communicate with Him. Although prayer is a spiritual mystery, He never intended it to be so mysterious that the process would be impossible or overly burdensome for us. Neither did He make it so spiritually complex that it could only be mastered by a few spiritual giants of the faith, nor so deep that it would require the kind of biblical comprehension of truth only lifetime theologians could discern.

His Word of Truth is easily accessed by anyone who searches for it with his or her whole heart. The Bible contains everything every believer needs to know about God, including how to confidently approach Him in prayer. The truth is there, hidden in plain view for those who have eyes to see and ears to hear. Jesus said that if we seek, we will find, and if we knock, the door will be opened. The question is how many of us are willing to truly seek truth with our whole hearts?

The Bible is a spiritual document, and the revelations it contains are invisible to the unregenerate eye. It can only be spiritually discerned by those who have been born of the Spirit. That is one of the reasons why Jesus sent Him to indwell us. As the Spirit of Truth, one of His assignments is to empower us to discern all spiritual truth, including everything we need to know about prayer.

Prayer might be a mystery, but it's no deep spiritual mystery to know that God dearly loves us. He made His love for us very plain by giving us His only begotten Son. Jesus is God's greatest expression of love. Through Christ, we receive every spiritual blessing. In Christ, we have everything we need for life and godliness.

God wants to have a rich, deep, ongoing spiritual relationship with us. He wants us to have complete confidence whenever we approach Him in prayer. Of course, He already knows our needs before we ask, but as a loving Father, He wants us to humbly bring our needs to Him so we can learn how faithful He is. But He doesn't want us to come only looking to get from Him. He also wants us to come desiring to give ourselves to Him.

> **Therefore, I urge you, brothers and sisters, in view of God's mercy, to offer your bodies as a living sacrifice, holy and pleasing to God—this is your true and proper worship.**
> **(Romans 12:1)**

The teachers of the law asked Jesus which commandment was the greatest.

> **Jesus replied: "Love the Lord your God with all your heart and with all your soul and with all your mind."**
> **(Matthew 22: 37)**

When we fervently search His Word with our whole heart, soul, and mind, it expresses love back to Him. It proves that His words matter to us, and we deeply care about what He deeply cares about. It says to Him, "I want Your kingdom to come and Your will to be done, on earth as it is in heaven." in accordance with the model prayer Jesus gave His disciples in Matthew 6:10.

Not only is this pleasing to Him, but by knowing and understanding the revelations of spiritual truth His Word clearly contains, we come to know His promises. Then we can pray confident prayers to Him in accordance with His will. He promised in 1 John 5:14 that these kinds of prayers will be heard and answered. When we pray to our loving Father in the name of His Son, He delights in hearing and answering those prayers because they're offered in the Spirit, in faith, and in truth.

Prayer Is a Conversation

Prayer in its most basic element is simply a conversation involving both talking and listening. But unlike natural conversations, this one is a vital, life-giving, and life-sustaining supernatural communication with God.

In prayer, listening to God is as important as talking to Him because prayer is a fluid exchange of sharing our hearts with a loving God and letting Him share His heart with us. After all, He's the one with the answers to all our questions. Maintaining healthy spiritual communion with Him in prayer provides the wisdom and insight needed for victorious Christian living and spiritual vitality.

Prayer Is a Spiritual Conversation

Prayer is not just talking at God. If we think that's what prayer is, there's a chance we may be talking but not being heard by God at all. Prayer in its most basic element is simply a conversation with our Creator, but what makes this conversation so unique is that it's happening in the Spirit realm.

To have a spiritual conversation, we must be spiritually connected. An unsaved person is spiritually dead in sins and separated from God. They have no spiritual access to talk to God. God is omnipresent, but when it comes to access to His spiritual kingdom, Jesus told this to Nicodemus in John 3:3, 5 that the only way to enter or see His kingdom is for a man to be born again by the Spirit.

The very instant we receive Christ as Savior, He takes our sins away and gives us His righteousness in exchange. We are instantly reborn, and His Spirit comes to live in us, sealing us and giving us unlimited access to His throne of grace through prayer. The Holy Spirit was also given to us to help us pray.

In the same way, the Spirit helps us in our weaknesses. We do not know what we ought to pray for, but the Spirit himself intercedes for us through wordless groans. And he who searches our hearts knows the mind of the Spirit, because the Spirit intercedes for God's people in accordance with the will of God. (Romans 8:26–27)

We must pray in the Holy Spirit because it takes spiritual power to make a spiritual connection with God in prayer. Being born again spiritually means having the Holy Spirit living in our human spirit. Trying to make a prayer connection with God without being in the Spirit is impossible.

Having a spiritual prayer connection is similar to the natural concept of needing both battery power and satellite connectivity to talk on your cell phone. Without a power source, the satellite connection is no good to you, and if your cell phone has power but no satellite access, you still can't get or receive a call.

The born-again human spirit is like our powered-up cell phone, and the Holy Spirit is like our satellite hookup to reach God. If we are trying to connect to God with our emotions and/or intellect (soulish nature) only, it's like having no power even though we have the Holy Spirit's indwelling (satellite hookup).

We can't get close to God with our human intellect! Intellect alone can't even begin to grasp the reality of God as Spirit. The spirit realm where God dwells can only be spiritually discerned. Unregenerate man cannot perceive it because of a spiritually dead condition:

> **The person without the Spirit does not accept the things that come from the Spirit of God but considers them foolishness, and cannot understand them because they are discerned only through the Spirit.**
> **(1 Corinthians 2:14)**

Praying in the Spirit means our human spirit is reaching out to God through the connecting power of the Holy Spirit. Only then can we "get a prayer through" as people like to say.

Being a Christian means we are in Christ and He is the only way to the Father. Jesus told His disciples He was going back to the Father to prepare a place for them but would be back to take them with Him. Thomas responded that they didn't know where He was going or how to get there.

> **Jesus answered, "I am the way and the truth and the life. No man comes to the Father, except through me"**
> **(John 14:6)**

Because we are in Christ, we have access to the Father by one Spirit. His blood continually cleanses us and His covering of righteousness over us makes it possible for us to go into the Holy of Holies. When the Father sees us, He doesn't see our fallen sin nature; He sees His Son's nature in us and His sacrifice for us. He sees Christ in us.

Prayer Is Worship

Saying, "Prayer is worship," may seem like a bit of an odd statement to some. We usually think of prayer and worship as two very separate activities, but actually, both are spiritual interactions with God. Many think of prayer as requesting something (physical/spiritual needs) from God, and they think of worship as giving something (praise/glory) to God.

God really needs nothing from anyone. He fills the universe. He is eternally complete, eternally full, and eternally holy. He is glorious and magnificent beyond measure. What does He need from anyone? It is for our benefit that He allows us to come into His presence and have relationship with Him. Because God is a consuming fire of power and glory, there is only one posture for going into the presence of God Almighty, and that posture is one of humble contrition, reverence, and worship covered in the righteousness of Christ Jesus.

That is why I consider both prayer and worship as relational in very nature. They are only possible through our relationship with Christ.

Prayer Is Communing with God

When most believers think of the word *communion*, we think of the ceremony we do the first Sunday in church of taking the bread and the wine. When Jesus first gave Communion to His disciples, it was during the Passover. He revealed Himself as the fulfilled meaning of the Passover feast. He said the bread was His body and the wine was His blood of the covenant poured out for many for the forgiveness of sins. He had told them earlier that unless they drank His blood and ate His flesh, they would have no life in themselves.

Then when they drew back, repelled by the idea, He explained that He wasn't talking about physically eating His flesh and drinking His blood. Jesus said the words He was speaking to them were spirit and life. Because He is eternal, His words are still as alive and spiritually powerful today as they were when He first spoke them. When we take Communion, He said we are to remember Him because it proclaims His death until He comes again. Communion is an intimate interaction with Him in mind and heart. When we do it, we are abiding in Him and He in us.

Communing with God in prayer is also a wonderful gift given by God to man as a means of communicating with Him. But a prerequisite to having a communal relationship with Him is to fully understand and apply the truth that since God gave us the best He had—Christ, His Son—He requires us to give all of ourselves to Him in total commitment.

True oneness of communion with Him can only happen when we reach out to Him in Christ with all of our heart and all of our soul and all of our mind. If we think we can approach Him in any other way, we are deceived. Whenever and however we commune with God, we are to examine ourselves and be discerning of His body. He knows us completely, and He easily recognizes halfhearted, superficial, faithless prayers.

Because God is love and He is truth, the only kinds of prayers that break through from the natural realm into the spiritual realm are the ones wrapped in love, faith in Christ, and the truth of His Word. True communal prayer is a very powerfully spiritual act of God, allowing us to participate in bringing His will to pass in our lives. But prayer is about much more than Him meeting just our needs. Through prayer, we can also be active participants in seeing God's will powerfully come to pass in meeting the needs in the lives of many others!

The communal interaction is confirmed when answers to prayer break through from the spiritual realm into the natural realm in manifestation. But we mustn't lose heart because of delayed manifestation. When we believe with all of our heart, soul, and mind that God loves us, and we know we have approached Him in accordance with His Word, the confidence of our communion with Him remains unbroken no matter what.

> **And without faith it is impossible to please God,
> because anyone who come to him must believe
> that he exists and that he rewards those who
> earnestly seek him.**
> (Hebrews 11:6)

Prayer Is Spiritual Warfare

Every Christian needs to know we are in a war. It is a battle of darkness against light. Diligent prayer is a powerfully dynamic weapon God gave every Christian to keep in his arsenal. He gave us the knowledge of how to use this weapon when we are doing kingdom work and come under attack by the Devil. The disciples' prayer says,

> **And lead us not into temptation, but deliver us
> from the evil one.**
> (Matthew 6:13).

This is a prayer for God's covering of protection from the access of evil and deliverance from it if we step out from under that covering and experience an attack. Not only has God given us His covering and weapons of defense, He also is our Deliverer!

There is a very well-known Scripture in the New Testament about those defensive weapons and how to use them for this battle. Many Christians have committed this Scripture to memory:

> **Finally, be strong in the Lord and in His mighty
> power. Put on the full armor of God, so that you
> can take your stand against the devil's schemes.
> For our struggle is not against flesh and blood,
> but against the rulers, against the authorities,
> against the powers of this dark world and against**

the spiritual forces of evil in the heavenly realms. Therefore put on the full armor of God, so that when the day of evil comes, you may be able to stand your ground, and after you have done everything, to stand. Stand firm then, with the belt of truth buckled around your waist, with the breastplate of righteousness in place, and with your feet fitted with the readiness that comes from the gospel of peace. In addition to all this, take up the shield of faith, with which you can extinguish all the flaming arrows of the evil one. Take the helmet of salvation and the sword of the Spirit, which is the word of God.
(Ephesians 6:10–17)

Most of us stop our memorization at verse 17, but the part I want to emphasize is the next verse. Although this piece of our armor is mentioned last, it certainly is not least in importance.

And pray in the Spirit on all occasions with all kinds of prayers and requests. With this in mind, be alert and always keep on praying for all the Lord's people.
(Ephesians 6:18)

The Evil One well knows the power of effectual, fervent prayer. His greatest hope is that we will never truly understand how to use the power of prayer effectively against his evil schemes. He uses every trick and distraction in his book of lies to try and keep believers from discovering truth from the Word of God. He doesn't want us to know that the power in prayer is founded and enforced by all that Christ accomplished for us on Calvary. The Devil as the Accuser of the brethren and doesn't want us to know and understand the truth about Jesus interceding for us as our High Priest.

> Therefore he is able to save completely those who come God through him, because he always lives to intercede for them.
> (Hebrews 7:25)

> Who then is the one who condemns? No one. Christ Jesus who died—more than that, who was raised to life—is at the right hand of God and is also interceding for us.
> (Romans 8:34)

> In the same way, the Spirit helps us in our weakness. We do not know what we ought to pray for, but the Spirit himself intercedes for us through wordless groans. And he who searches our hearts knows the mind of the Spirit, because the Spirit intercedes for God's people in accordance with the will of God.
> (Romans 8:26–27)

The Devil fears that if we begin to realize the power of the intercession of Jesus and the Holy Spirit and how much power has been given us by praying the Word in Jesus' name, we will learn how to defeat him. We will begin to pray fervent, truth-based, confident prayers to get God's will accomplished on the earth. There is no doubt we are at war, but we have been well equipped to fight!

> For though we live in the world, we do not wage war as the world does. The weapons we fight with are not the weapons of the world. On the contrary, they have divine power to demolish strongholds. We demolish arguments and every pretension that sets itself up against the

knowledge of God, and we take captive every
thought to make it obedient to Christ.
(2 Corinthians 10:3–5)

What Is a Stronghold?

A stronghold is a fortification or fortress, a powerful hiding place
of security, protection and refuge against an enemy. Paul explains
the usage of the word *stronghold* in this context as pertaining to evil
things standing in opposition to truth. Since we know that the Devil
is a liar and the father of all lies, there is no doubt he is the source of
all these lying fortresses of arguments and pretenses that go against
the knowledge of God.

The word *stronghold* in this context can also be explained as
intellectually arrogant obstacles; lofty opinions; high things;
imaginations; carnal reasoning; disputations against truth; proud
thoughts of heart; swelling words of vanity; haughtiness of men.

All of these definitions expose strongholds as demonically
inspired reasoning and lies intended to oppose the light of truth.
Have you ever considered that the following are established and
enforced by strongholds?

- sickness
- poverty
- depression
- fear
- anger
- unforgiveness
- anxiety
- all kinds of addictions

These things are all curses, and they are both established and
reinforced by believing some kind of a lie. Since the outcome is that

these things steal, kill, and destroy lives, do you have any doubt where the lie that they are fed on originates?

I believe there are dark spirits assigned to each of these curses. They are lying familiar spirits, and their assignment is to draw weak people into the spiritual darkness of the dysfunction they are familiar with so that a stronghold can be built up. The lies they use to do this are very seductive and deceitful.

These familiar spirits don't come draped in darkness saying, "Follow me. I'm a dark, familiar spirit from the pits of hell, who hates you. My job is to do everything in my power to keep you from trusting God for healing, deliverance, and restoration. I don't want you to find God's will for your life and be blessed. I want you to live in despair and hopelessness. I despise the thought of your prosperity, peace, and good health. I want to entrap your soul in pain and misery in total darkness until I can completely destroy your life.

"Come on, you know this prison of pain already. It's very familiar to you and you've grown comfortable in it, haven't you? Doesn't it feel safe like a shelter? There are no surprises here. At least you know what to expect. Don't take the risk of faith and hope. You will only be disappointed, again. You might as well just accept this situation. I'm telling you this because I'm your friend and just want you to listen to me. Face the facts: this is your lot in life, so stop fighting it. Fighting against the facts is pointless."

You might find this hard to accept, but the curses listed above are all addictive. The more familiar we become with a curse, the more enslaved to the addiction we become until the dysfunction becomes an entrenchment built up into a powerful stronghold. The walls of this prison are built up of lies fortified by layers of familiar emotional scar tissue reinforced to stop truth and healing from getting in. They keep the individual suffering from this dysfunction as a captive trapped in. After a while, a sense of hopeless sets in with the feeling that change is impossible.

Of course this is a lie! Nothing is impossible with God! Jesus came to set the captive free. He has given us mighty weapons of faith and speaking the Word of God that can demolish these strongholds. But before a stronghold can be torn down, we have to be willing to breach the threshold of pain that has been surrounding it to keep us captive. If strongholds are established and reinforced by lies, then only truth can tear them down!

To demolish strongholds of darkness and lies, we must use the sword of the Spirit, which is the Word of God, full of life, light, and truth. What does God's Word say about?

> *Sickness.* **"But he was pierced for our transgressions, he was crushed for our iniquities; the punishment that brought us peace was on him, and by his wounds we are healed."**
> **(Isaiah 53:5)**

> *Poverty.* **"For you know the grace of our Lord Jesus Christ, that though he was rich, yet for your sake he became poor, so that you through his poverty might become rich."**
> **(2 Corinthians 8:9)**

> *Depression.* **"Why, my soul, are you downcast? Why so disturbed with me? Put your hope in God for I will yet praise him, my Savior and my God."**
> **(Psalm 42:11)**

> *Fear.* **"When I am afraid, I put my trust in you. In God, whose word I praise—in God I trust and am not afraid. What can mere mortals do to me?"**
> **(Psalm 56:3–4)**

Anger. "Refrain from anger and turn from wrath; do not fret—it leads only to evil." (Psalm 37:8)

Unforgiveness. "Be kind and compassionate to one another, forgiving each other, just as in Christ God forgave you." (Ephesians 4:32)

Anxiety. "Cast all your anxiety on him because he cares for you." (1 Peter 5:7)

All kinds of addictions. "For the grace of God has appeared that offers salvation to all people. It teaches us to say 'No' to ungodliness and worldly passions, and to live self-controlled, upright and godly lives in this present age, while we wait for the blessed hope—the appearing of the glory of our great God and Savior, Jesus Christ, who gave himself for us to redeem us from all wickedness and to purify for himself a people that are his very own, eager to do what is good." (Titus 2:11–14)

The power of truth will demolish every lie! We must remember that strongholds are not just an external concept. The verse we read in 2 Corinthians 10:5 about demolishing lies that come against the knowledge of God and taking thoughts captive to make them obedient to Christ is talking about lying thoughts and ideas wherever they may exist, especially in our own minds. We can only take our own thoughts captive, not another person's. False teachers can present false doctrine and try to build up a stronghold of lies, but each individual determines if he or she will accept or reject those lies. It is up to each of us to bring every thought and imagining into obedience to Christ so that no stronghold of lies can be allowed to build up in our own minds.

We have examined the strongholds (fortresses of darkness), but that isn't the only way those concepts are used in Scripture. Scripture shows that there are also fortresses or strongholds of light in God's kingdom.

> **The Lord is my rock, my fortress and my deliverer, my God is my rock, in whom I take refuge, my shield and the horn of my salvation, my stronghold.**
> **(Psalm 18:2)**

> **Truly he is my rock and my salvation; he is my fortress, I will not be shaken.**
> **(Psalm 62:6)**

> **He is my loving God and my fortress, my stronghold and my deliverer, my shield, in whom I take refuge, who subdues peoples under me.**
> **(Psalm 144:2)**

We find our safety and security in the stronghold of God and His truth. In God's stronghold of light, the Devil's lies are easily identified, and we give his lies no hiding place in our thoughts. With our full armor on—the helmet of salvation to protect our minds and the sword of the Spirit in one hand and the shield of faith in the other—we take our stand against the Devil's schemes, and we extinguish all his evil flaming arrows. When we resist the Devil, he has no choice. He must flee! This verse is worth repeating and repeating and repeating!

> **For though we live in the world, we do not wage war as the world does. The weapons we fight**

> **with are not the weapons of the world. On the contrary, they have divine power to demolish strongholds.**
>
> **(2 Corinthians 10:3–4)**

Prayer

Thank You, Father, that the power that raised Christ Jesus from the dead lives in us! No weapon formed against us will prosper, because we are strong in You, Lord, and in the power of Your might. Show us how to bring all lying strongholds down in Jesus' holy name. Amen!

CHAPTER 7

Different Kinds of Prayer

I n Ephesians 6:18, Paul told them to pray on all occasions with all kinds of prayers and requests, so part of our prayer revolution is erudition on the different kinds of prayers. **Philippians 4:6** says,

> **"Do not be anxious about anything, but in every situation, by prayer and petition, with thanksgiving, present your requests to God."**

Ephesians 6:18 says,

> **And pray in the Spirit on all occasions with all kinds of prayers and requests.**

The very concept that prayer is communion and a literal conversation with God is in itself a paradigm shift for some. It is a revolutionary change in their perception of what constitutes a relationship with God.

We understand conversations well enough when it has to do with other people. Conversations flow depending on what one intends to communicate. You may have something very specific in mind when you call a loved one. There are times you get right to the point and other times when you work your way up to it. Just like there are different focuses in conversations with other people, it's no different in our conversations with God.

The two Scripture references above make it clear there are different elements or focuses in prayer, and they are all important:

- worship and praise
- thanksgiving
- confession and repentance
- supplication/petition/requests
- intercession

I realize all of these can be in one prayer, but there are also times one in particular can be a primary focus. Worship, praise, and thanksgiving are a natural response to being in His presence, but the others don't have to necessarily be a part of every prayer. I know this statement might not be well received by some, but please remember that prayer is a flowing, honest conversation with God. It is a special time when we go before Him to share what is in our hearts and hear what is in His. If your heart is full of one of these, reverently go into His presence and pour it out. God wants honesty. Forced formality and ritual in prayer is counterproductive.

David's prayers in the Psalms run the full gamut. Maybe it would be helpful to read a few of them if you're still doubtful. David had a very special relationship with God. He was far from being a perfect man, but God said that David was a man after His own heart. Even so, David also made more than one prayer of complaint toward God in the Psalms.

I didn't put a prayer of "complaint" on my list because being in Christ, we don't have to even go there. His goodness always leads those who love Him to repentance, and His truth always sets us free from wrong thinking. His truth has the power to renew our minds. When we open our hearts to receive it, we can know what His good, acceptable, and perfect will is for our lives.

Jabez's prayer in 1 Chronicles 4:10 is a perfect example of a single-focus prayer. Jabez had one objective in his short prayer: supplication. The outcome is clear because God heard his prayer and granted his request. We will look more closely at Jabez's prayer a bit later on.

If you're walking through a deep valley and the honest attitude of your heart is a complaint toward God because you just can't seem to make any sense out of your circumstances, why not take this time in prayer to share it reverently to God in a prayer of confession and repentance.

Prayer

God, I know You are omniscient and already know how I feel anyway. I believe You always want me to come to You in truth. That means You want me to be honest with You about all of my feelings both good and bad. Thank You, Lord, for not rejecting me for being honest with You. I know that You love me and want me to bring You all my cares so that You can heal my broken heart.

Thank You for healing me right now and filling me up with Your joy. I turn away from all bitterness and unforgiveness. Please show me the truth about my circumstances and help me trust that Your hand will guide me through it all. In Jesus' name. Amen.

*****

The Disciples Prayer

When the disciples asked Jesus to teach them to pray, He gave them a prayer, which most know as the Lord's Prayer.

> **And when you pray, do not be like the hypocrites,**
> **for they love to pray standing in the synagogues**

and on the street corners to be seen by others. Truly I tell you, they have received their reward in full. But when you pray, go into your room, close the door and pray to your Father, who is unseen. Then your Father, who sees what is done in secret, will reward you. And when you pray, do not keep on babbling like pagans, for they think they will be heard because of their many words. Do not be like them, for your Father knows what you need before you ask Him. This, then, is how you should pray: Our Father in heaven, hallowed be your name, your kingdom come, your will be done, on earth as it is in heaven. Give us today our daily bread. And forgive us our debts, as we have also forgiven our debtors. And lead us not into temptation, but deliver us from the evil one. For if you forgive others when they sin against you, your heavenly Father will also forgive you.
(Matthew 6:5–14)

Now, let's unpack this prayer a little bit.

"Our Father in Heaven"

In the beginning God created the heavens and the earth.
(Genesis 1:1)

Then God said, "Let us make man in our image, in our likeness.... So God created man in his own image, in the image of God he created him; male and female he created them."
(Genesis 1:26–27)

God is Spirit. He created a man and a woman and breathed life into them. The life He breathed into them was spirit. He is the God of truth, and as Creator, He is the Father of *all* mankind. Whether we want relationship with Him or not doesn't change the truth that He is our Father.

> **Moreover, we have all had human fathers who disciplined us and we respected them for it. How much more should we submit to the Father of spirits and live.**
> **(Hebrews 12:9)**

"Hallowed Be Your Name"

Hallowed means honored as holy. To honor as holy is to show respect and to esteem Him as divine, exalted, worthy of reverence, sacred. So what's in a name? In the days of the Bible, a person's name represented who they were. It spoke of their family and their character. A name was like a label.

God's name represents His being, His magnificence in power, glory, and truth. Many Jews hallowed His name so much that they wouldn't even speak or spell it out. In this prayer, Jesus is saying God's name is to be honored and considered holy. Names mean little or nothing today for the most part. People often label their child with a name for the silliest of reasons or even as a joke. As a result of that, some children come into this world with a label of disrespect they have to cope with until they're old enough to change it. So it's no surprise that today the irreverent commonly use God's name as a curse word and don't give it a thought. The honor and holiness of God's name means absolutely nothing to the lost because their spirits are disconnected from Him by sin.

> **You shall not misuse the name of the Lord your God, for the Lord will not hold anyone guiltless who misuses his name.**
> **(Deuteronomy 5:11)**

The Devil has blinded the minds of unbelievers so that they can't see His holiness and the glory reflected in His Son, Jesus, and so they dishonor Him with both their words and their lives. To dishonor the Father is to dishonor the Son, and to dishonor the Son is to dishonor the Father:

"I and the Father are one."
(John 10:30)

It is the Father who exalted the name of Jesus.

Therefore God exalted him to the highest place and gave him the name that is above very name, that at the name of Jesus every knee should bow, in heaven and on earth and under the earth and every tongue acknowledge that Jesus Christ is Lord, to the glory of God the Father.
(Philippians 2:9–11)

Salvation is found in no one else, for there is no other name given under heaven given to mankind by which we must be saved.
(Acts 4:12)

God's name has power attached to it when used by His authority. When He sent the Old Testament prophets to the Jews, He sent them to prophecy in His name. When Jesus came to earth, He spoke in the Father's name and did the work He was sent to do. When He returned to His Father, He sent the church out into the world to continue His work and gave us approval to use His name to accomplish His will. Here are a few Scriptures from the New Testament about the authority of using His name:

And these signs will accompany those who
believe: In my name they will drive out demons;
they will speak in new tongues;
(Mark 16:17)

And I will do whatever you ask in my name, so
that the Father may be glorified in the Son. You
may ask me for anything in my name, and I will
do it.
(John 14:13–14)

In that day you will no longer ask me anything.
Very truly I tell you, my Father will give you
whatever you ask in my name.
(John 16:23)

Jesus warned that in the last days much persecution will also
come on account of His name but according to Luke 21:12 at the
end of time, all men will be forced to bow their knee to God and
hallow His name whether they want to or not.

"Your Kingdom Come"

When Jesus came into the world, He went around teaching the good
news of the kingdom. He taught on it everywhere He went, and His
teachings are well noted in all the Gospels. However, today there is
a lot of confusion about the subject of the kingdom. Before we can
understand God's kingdom, we must first realize there are actually
three kingdoms actively at work at this time fighting for dominance
and power to control men's souls.

1. *God's kingdom of light*
    a. Christ reigns as King.
    b. God's kingdom is made up of redeemed men (the
       church). (Note: The angelic forces are subjects

purposed to do His bidding by caring for kingdom citizens. According to John 3:5, only those born of water—i.e., humans and the Spirit—can actually enter the kingdom.)

2. *Satan's kingdom of darkness*
   a. The Devil reigns as king.
   b. Demons inhabit this kingdom and accomplish Satan's agenda by using men who have yielded themselves over to the powers of darkness.

3. *The kingdoms of this world*
   a. Men rule this kingdom.
   b. This is human government in whatever form it exists. It is the world's system of power and control.

In regard to God's kingdom, there seem to be three basic trains of thought in Christian circles that teach about the nature and timing of it:

1. *God's kingdom is only physical* (denies any spiritual application).
   a. The coming of the kingdom is strictly a future event. It is not currently here and will not come until Christ's second coming.
   b. "Kingdom Now" theology. This is a physical-only concept taken to an extreme. The kingdom is physically here already and advocates efforts toward establishing a Christian theocracy, right now.

2. *God's kingdom is only spiritual* (denies any physical application).
   Everything in the book of Revelation should be spiritualized.

3. *God's kingdom is both spiritual and physical.*
   a. The spiritual kingdom is present in the church, here and now.

    b. The physical kingdom is coming at the second coming of Christ.

    c. The book of Revelation has both spiritual and physical applications.

Since we know Jesus is the King and it is His kingdom, before deciding whether 1, 2, or 3 is correct, let's consider what the King taught about His kingdom. Then we can correctly understand what He meant in the disciples' prayer we are studying when He said, **"Your kingdom come."**

Jesus taught:

> **Repent, for the kingdom of heaven has come near.**
> **(Matthew 4:17)**

> **The law and the Prophets were proclaimed until John. Since that time, the good news of the kingdom of God is being preached, and everyone is forcing his way into it.**
> **(Luke 16:16)**

> **He said, "The knowledge of the secrets of the kingdom of God has been given to you, but to others I speak in parables, so that,**
> **though seeing they may not see, though hearing, they may not understand.**
> **(Luke 8:10)**

> **"Truly I tell you, some who are standing here will not taste death before they see the kingdom of God."**
> **(Luke 9:27)**

Consider how the wild flowers grow. They do not labor or spin. Yet I tell you, not even Solomon in all his splendor was dressed like one of these. If that is how God clothes the grass of the field, which is here today, and tomorrow is thrown into the fire, how much more will he clothe you—you of little faith! And do not set your heart on what you will eat or drink; do not worry about it. For the pagan world runs after all such things, and your Father knows that you need them. But seek his kingdom, and these things will be given to you as well.
(Luke 12:27–31)

Once, on being asked by the Pharisees when the kingdom of God would come, Jesus replied, "The coming of the kingdom of God is not something that can be observed, nor will people say, 'Here it is' or 'There it is,' because the kingdom of God is in your midst."
(Luke 17:20–21)

Jesus replied, "Very truly I tell you, no one can see the kingdom of God unless they are born again."
(John 3:3)

Jesus answered, "Very truly I tell you, no one can enter the kingdom of God unless they are born of water and the Spirit."
(John 3:5)

Jesus said, "My kingdom is not of this world. If it were, my servants would fight to prevent

my arrest by the Jewish leaders. But now my
kingdom is from another place."
(John 18:36)

After His ascension, the apostles continued His teaching:

**For the kingdom of God is not a matter of eating
and drinking, but of righteousness, peace, and
joy in the Holy Spirit.
(Romans 14:17)**

**For the kingdom of God is not a matter of talk
but of power.
(1 Corinthians 4:20)**

**For he has rescued us from the dominion of
darkness and brought us into the kingdom of
the Son he loves.
(Colossians 1:13 (TNIV)**

**Listen, my dear brothers and sisters: Has God
not chosen those who are poor in the eyes of
the world to be rich in faith and to inherit the
kingdom he promised those who love him?
(James 2:5)**

**The seventh angel sounded his trumpet, and
there were loud voices in heaven, which said:
"The kingdom of the world has become the
kingdom of our Lord and of his Messiah and he
will reign forever and ever."
(Revelation 11:15)**

Now let's consider what these verses teach us about God's kingdom:

- It came to earth in Christ, the King.
- It began to be forcefully advanced and laid hold of by men from the time of the preaching of John the Baptist.
- It has secrets that only His chosen can know.
- Now, it is an invisible, spiritual kingdom that is not of this world, but only seen spiritually by those who have been born again.
- Only those born of water and of the Holy Spirit can enter it.
- It is a powerful kingdom of righteousness, peace, and joy in the Holy Spirit.
- Christians, already citizens of Christ's spiritual kingdom, are to "seek first the kingdom of God and His righteousness." When we do, He has promised to take care of our physical needs.
- In the future, it will be a visible, physical kingdom reigned over by King Jesus at His second coming, and we will reign with Him.
- Christians have an inheritance in Christ's future physical kingdom. This part of the kingdom will come at His second coming when He puts down all other kingdoms and reigns over the whole earth.

Based on these teachings, it is clear to me the correct way to understand the nature and timing of God's kingdom is the third interpretation as both spiritual and physical. God's *spiritual* kingdom is both real and powerful. Perhaps that is why Christ spent so much time teaching on it at His first coming.

Before He left, He commissioned His church to go into the entire world and preach the good news of the kingdom of God as He did when He was on earth. When the church was birthed on the day of Pentecost, Jesus sent the Holy Spirit to guide and empower the church to fulfill the mission of forcefully advancing His *spiritual* kingdom by growing it daily with new births from every nation, tribe, and tongue.

King Jesus is powerfully reigning right now as Lord and King in His church and in the individual lives of believers. Citizens of God's kingdom, yielding to the indwelling Holy Spirit, listen and obey His commands and continually seek to advance His kingdom agenda.

Christ's second coming will be a future *physical* return to the earth. At that time, He will establish His *physical* kingdom on the earth in power and great glory just as He promised in His Word, and the faithful will reign with Him on earth.

The kingdom of God contains many secrets and deep truths that are not easy to understand. The Bible reveals some of these truths to us, but there is much we don't know. I believe that as we grow in spiritual maturity, understanding, and obeying what we do know, the Holy Spirit will reveal more to us.

"Your Will Be Done"

When God created mankind, He gave us the precious gift of free will. He could have created us without the capability to resist His will, but in perfect wisdom, He gave man the right to freely choose to love and obey Him. Being omniscient, it was no surprise when Adam and Eve misused their free will to disobey Him by eating from the forbidden tree. He knew before He created them that they would do just that.

The Tree of Knowledge of Good and Evil was the only thing forbidden in the garden. Some wonder why He created that tree so beautiful and allowed it to be within reach. He could have made it disgusting to sight and smell or covered it with thorns, but those qualities are normally associated with death or decay, and the garden was full of life. Death, decay, and thorns came about after the fall in the world outside the garden.

Besides, what good is free will without a choice of options? The Tree of Life was also there within reach; it had the ability to give eternal life. I imagine it was also as desirable, but it was not forbidden to them. God clearly warned them that the day they ate from the forbidden tree, "you will surely die."

I wonder what would have happened if they had obeyed God's will, resisted the Serpent, and chosen to eat from the Tree of Life instead. Perhaps, they would have become more like God, knowing perfect good without ever experiencing the evil of disobedience, sin, and death. But that is not how it happened. The Serpent convinced them of the vile lie that eating from the Tree of Knowledge of Good and Evil would be a good thing to do because it would give them power to be like God. As silly as it sounds, he convinced them that disobeying God was the best way to attain godliness, and that knowing evil was good.

God's will was for Adam and Eve to remain in unhindered relationship with Him, but they abused their gift of free will by turning away from the giver of life. They turned toward death and submitted themselves to the will of the Devil. When they did, the dominion over the creation God had given to Adam was subjugated to the Devil.

But God always had a plan, and man's sin did not catch Him off guard. He didn't wring His hands and say, "Oh my, man has sinned. Son, whatever shall we do now?" No God knew, for the Bible says in Revelation 13:8, "The Lamb who was slain from the creation of the world." From the creation of the world, God knew He would send His Son to make sure His will would be done on earth as it was in heaven.

For God so loved the world that he gave his one and only Son, that whosoever believes in him should not perish but have eternal life. (John 3:16)

God's will to have unhindered relationship with men would be made possible by the sacrifice of His Son!

When we give our lives to Christ, He gives us the gift of the Holy Spirit, enabling us with the power to turn away from sinful bad choices and to know, love, and obey God's will instead. From that point, God's will, not ours, is what should be most important to us. His will is to fulfill His plans and His purpose in our lives. His Word reveals His will to us, and by studying it with a yielded heart, the Holy Spirit helps us discover what He wants for us and from us. It lets us know He has big plans for our lives!

> **"For I know the plans I have for you," declares the Lord, "plans to prosper you and not to harm you, plans to give you hope and a future."**
> **(Jeremiah 29:11)**

> **Give thanks in all circumstances; for this is God's will for you in Christ Jesus.**
> **(1 Thessalonians 5:18)**

> **For it is God's will that by doing good you should silence the ignorant talk of foolish people.**
> **(1 Peter 2:15)**

> **The Lord is not slow in keeping his promise, as some understand slowness. He is patient with you, not wanting anyone to perish, but everyone to come to repentance.**
> **(2 Peter 3:9)**

> **You need to persevere so that when you have done the will of God, you will receive what he has promised.**
> **(Hebrews 10:36)**

> **It's God's will that you should be sanctified: that you should avoid sexual immorality.**
> **(1 Thessalonians 4:3)**

> **Do not conform to the pattern of this world, but be transformed by the renewing of your mind. Then you will be able to test and approve what God's will is—his good, pleasing and perfect will.**
> **(Romans 12:2)**

"On Earth as It Is in Heaven."

The first book of the Bible tells us clearly that God created the earth and the heavens. Since He created everything, it is all His to do with as He pleases.

> **To the Lord your God belong the heavens, even the highest heavens, the earth and everything on it.**
> **(Deuteronomy 10:14)**

God created the earth and man who lives on it; His creation declares His power by simply existing, and His glory floods heaven. He is the Lord God of heaven. He rules over heaven above and earth below from His magnificent throne, and Jesus sits at His right hand. The angels and the multitudes of heavenly beings never cease worshipping Him.

> **The heavens declare the glory of God; the skies proclaim the work of his hands.**
> **(Psalms 19:1)**

Acknowledge and take to heart this day that the Lord is God in heaven above and on the earth below. There is no other.
(Deuteronomy 4:39)

Yours, Lord, is the greatness and the power and the glory and the majesty and the splendor, for everything in heaven and earth is yours. Yours, Lord, is the kingdom; you are exalted as head over all.
(1 Chronicles 29:11)

The Lord looks down from heaven on all mankind to see if there are any who understand, any who seek God.
(Psalm 14:2)

The Lord has established his throne in heaven, and his kingdom rules over all.
(Psalm 103:19)

Heaven must receive him until the time comes for God to restore everything, as he promised long ago through his holy prophets.
(Acts 3:21)

He made known to us the mystery of his will according to his good pleasure, which he purposed in Christ, to be put into effect when the times reach their fulfillment—to bring unity to all things in heaven and on earth under Christ.
(Ephesians 1:9–10)

> **But in keeping with his promise we are looking
> forward to a new heaven and a new earth, where
> righteousness dwells.**
> **(2 Peter 3:13)**

The Bible reveals both the beginning and the end of time. God said His creation was good because life began in perfection. It tells us how sin tainted His creation and how He will finally renew it back to its original state of perfection. He is God over all the kingdoms of the earth, and soon He will come as judge. In the end, heaven and earth will be one.

"Give Us Today Our Daily Bread"

God as our loving Father cares about our needs and tells us not to be anxious about them. He sustains the universe by His power. Since He fills the universe, He is more than able to take care of us. Many of us have great difficulty simply living in the moment, only concerning ourselves with our daily needs. It seems cavalier or very careless not to worry about tomorrow's needs.

> **So do not worry, saying, "What shall we eat?" or
> "What shall we drink?" or "what shall we wear?"
> For the pagans run after all these things, and
> your heavenly Father knows that you need them.
> But seek first his kingdom and his righteousness
> and all these things shall be added to you as well.
> (Matthew 6:31–33)**

> **And my God will meet all your needs according
> to his glorious riches in Christ Jesus.
> (Philippians 4:19)**

"And Forgive Us Our Debts, as We Have Forgiven Our Debtors"

Because Adam was our forefather, we inherited his human nature and were born debtors to God because of sin. It was a debt we could never pay. That is why Jesus came to pay our sin debt with the sacrifice of His precious blood. He gave His life to purchase eternal forgiveness for us, rose from the dead, and is right now sitting at the Father's right hand making intercession for us. Because He is there, we can be sure the flow of forgiveness is always available to us. It's a river of living water that flows from God's mercy seat to all who are in Christ.

This river of forgiveness consists of a healing flow of truth and love that heals us and then flows through us to heal others. The more it flows through us, the more of it He flows to us. This flow is a spiritual reality that is consistent with every blessing we receive from God. Everything we receive comes to us because of our position in Christ. We could never work long enough or perfect enough to earn what is only available by grace. He gives to us freely so we can give freely to others.

Works can't earn God's forgiveness, love, or favor. It can only come by grace through faith in Christ. How then can we think others must work to earn our forgiveness, love, or favor by what they do for us? An attitude like this is not based on truth or love. What takes grace to receive must be given by grace to others.

Just as we received forgiveness freely, we must give it freely. We have to let the forgiveness from God flow down from heaven like a river of living water. We must let it do its work in us, cleansing us completely with truth and love, and then we must let it flow through us freely to others. What is that cleansing truth?

> that God was reconciling the world to himself
> in Christ, not counting people's sins against
> them. And he has committed to us the message
> of reconciliation.
> (2 Corinthians 5:19)

What is that cleansing love?

> **For I am convinced that neither death nor life,
> neither angels nor demons, neither the present
> nor the future, nor any powers, neither height
> nor depth, nor anything else in all creation, will
> be able to separate us from the love of God that
> is in Christ Jesus our Lord.**
> **(Romans 8:38–39)**

"And Lead Us Not into Temptation"

I have to admit; this part of the prayer was very hard to comprehend. I couldn't understand why Jesus would have told them to ask the Father such a question. There was a lot I didn't understand about the first part, "and lead us not into," so I directed my attention to "temptation."

> **Then Jesus was led by the Spirit into the
> wilderness to be tempted by the devil.**
> **(Matthew 4:1)**

> **When tempted, no one should say, "God is
> tempting me." For God cannot be tempted by
> evil, nor does he tempt anyone; but each person
> is tempted when they are dragged away by their
> own evil desire and enticed.**
> **(James 1:13–14)**

> **For this reason he had to be made like them,
> fully human in every way, in order that he
> might become a merciful and faithful high
> priest in service to God, and that he might make
> atonement for the sins of the people. Because he**

himself suffered when he was tempted, he is able
to help those who are being tempted.
(Hebrews 2:17–18)

For we do not have a high priest who is unable
to empathize with our weaknesses, but we have
one who has been tempted in every way, just as
we are—yet he did not sin.
(Hebrews 4:15)

I saw a universal theme in these verses. The Devil is the tempter and God is the one who helps and delivers us when we are tempted and call on Him. God is the one who provides a way of escape. The Devil could never have succeeded in tempting Jesus. Jesus could have easily cast the Devil away from Him in an instant!

So why did the Holy Spirit lead Jesus into temptation in the wilderness? He did it for us! Everything Jesus did while walking the earth was modeling for us how we are also to walk. Jesus was led into the wilderness for forty days like the children of Israel were led into the wilderness for forty years. He succeeded where they failed.

His victory over temptation showed us He could fully empathize with our human weaknesses. He overcame temptation at the point of intense human weakness and proved He was God in the flesh, perfect in holiness. As He said to His disciples, so He says to us today, **"Follow Me."**

Temptations will come in this life because we are human. The Devil knows the weakness of human flesh, so he is constantly sending the forces of hell to tempt our human nature to sin. The lusts of the flesh, the lust of the eyes, and the pride of life are his targets for seduction. His lie is that these things have the power to satisfy us. That is exactly what he used against Adam and Eve in the garden and what he tried to use to tempt Jesus in the wilderness.

The Devil's methods have not changed since he fell, but neither has the power of God's Word changed! If Eve had responded to the

Devil's temptation to eat from the forbidden tree by simply repeating what God had said and turned away from him, his temptation would have failed. Instead, she stayed, listened to the Devil's twisted lies, believed them, and sinned.

The Bible refers to Jesus as the "last Adam." He came into the world to pay the sin debt initiated by the first Adam's fall. He also came to model the right way to respond to Satan's temptation. It was the truth of God's Word that Jesus spoke to defeat the Devil, and it will be the truth of God's Word that we must speak to deliver us from the Devil's tempting lies. It will deliver us the same way it delivered Christ. The Bible says, "Resist the devil and he will flee," and we resist him by speaking, "It is written …" in response to his speaking lies.

Jesus laid down the power of His divinity, took on human flesh, then walked every day of His earthly ministry under the power and control of the Holy Spirit. He never acted independently but taught that He only said and did what He heard His Father say and saw His Father do.

The Spirit of God led Jesus into the wilderness to be tempted. He did it for our sake, providing us with an example to follow when we are tempted. So if Jesus told His disciples to ask the Father to "lead us not into temptation," we must consider it a possibility that sometime in our lives, the Spirit may lead us into temptation.

And if the Spirit does lead us there, we must remember Jesus' example and His admonition to pick up our own cross and follow Him. He has promised to never leave us or forsake us. He empathizes with us and will help us. He will not allow any temptation to be greater than what we can bear and will work all things together for our good. When one of us gets the victory over the Devil's temptation, our example is an encouragement to other believers that they can do the same, and God is glorified in it all.

No temptation has overtaken you except what is common to mankind. And God is faithful;

he will not let you be tempted beyond what you can bear. But when you are tempted, he will also provide a way out so you can endure it.
(1 Corinthians 10:13)

"Deliver Us from the Evil One"

And if he rescued Lot, a righteous man, who was distressed by the depraved conduct of the lawless (for that righteous man, living among them, day after day, was tormented in his righteous soul by the lawless deeds he saw and heard)—if this is so, then the Lord knows how to rescue the godly from trials and to hold the unrighteous for punishment on the day of judgment.
(2 Peter 2:7–9)

Jesus defeated the Devil and powerfully lives in us. Jesus is the Word made flesh. He is the truth, and He is the life. Every time we speak God's truth, the very life-giving power of what Jesus accomplished by His life, death and resurrection will always defeat darkness and deliver us from the Evil One.

God is the mighty deliverer. He was, He is, and He will forever be the deliverer of all who put their trust in Him.

"For if You Forgive Other People When They Sin against You, Your Heavenly Father Will Also Forgive You"

As we look at this part of the prayer, we can see how serious forgiveness is to God. He gave His Son to provide it to us. Forgiveness is meant to flow like a living river. If it flows to us then out to others, it is full of life and healing, but if it is not allowed to flow outward to others, the lack of forward movement causes forgiveness to be cut off from its life source, God. Disconnected from truth and love, forgiveness becomes like the Dead Sea. It is void of the power needed to sustain life.

Unforgiveness is an extremely toxic emotion. It can saturate the soul, and if allowed to remain, will develop into a root of bitterness.

**Get rid of all bitterness, rage and anger, brawling and slander, along with every form of malice. Be kind and compassionate to one another, forgiving each other, just as in Christ God forgave you.
(Ephesians 4:31–32)**

Unforgiveness defiles many and is the root cause of much sickness and even death in those who continue in it. So we need to be honest with ourselves and understand what nurtures unforgiveness in us before we can deal with it. I have come to understand there is a direct connection and correlation between these two conflicting emotional states:

- Unforgiveness and the brokenness (of body and mind)
- Forgiveness and healing

Whenever we are sinking in the mire of unforgiveness, it's because we are clinging to and nurturing the memory of an offense, refusing to release the offender. I often wonder why it's so hard to forgive an offense. We all have been guilty of being the offender. We all have offended another person in word or deed at one time or another. Sometimes an offense is intended, sometimes it is accidental, but an offense is an offense. It still causes injury, regardless of motive. It is battery against the soul and wounds.

Some wounds can go very deep, especially if the offense hits a place of sensitivity caused by a prior injury. If that prior injury is still unhealed and raw, and another person's offense against us hits the target of that sensitive spot, the wound goes even deeper and exacerbates the painful damage already done. The additional wounding received leaves even less chance of healing. If the prior injury had only partially healed, it is freshly reopened by the new offense.

When we refuse to forgive ourselves for our imperfections and personal failures, guilt and shame cause us to punish ourselves. We batter ourselves, then unwisely justify our own suffering from these self-injuries and self-offenses as deserved. What's worse is to accuse God of being the one who is behind the punishment. By doing that, we also deny forgiveness to ourselves from Him and cut off the healing that receiving His forgiveness delivers.

Under these conditions, the wound is kept in a perpetually raw state as we continue battering and abusing ourselves with constant negative self-talk fueled by our poor self-image. Those unwilling to forgive themselves also struggle to forgive others. The symptom of suffering with the spiritual malady of unforgiveness is brokenness of mind and body, and embracing the truth is the only way to be healed and set free.

Forgiveness is the heart of the gospel. We were all separated from God because we all have been guilty of offending God by sinning against Him. All offense is against His holiness; it is a sin against the Lord. So the truth is, we are all guilty! We all inherited Adam's sin nature; so sinning comes natural to us. We had no possible way on our own to kick our sin addiction and find forgiveness with Him.

> **Indeed, there is no one on earth who is righteous, no one who does what is right and never sins. (Ecclesiastes 7:20)**
>
> **for all have sinned and fall short of the glory of God. (Romans 3:23)**

Separation from God by our sins and offenses with no ability within us to change left us in a hopeless condition. We were hell bound.

> **The wages of sin is death, but the gift of God is eternal life in Christ Jesus our Lord.**
> **(Romans 6:23)**

So God had to make a way to set us free from slavery to sin so we could be forgiven and have fellowship with Him. He sent His Son into the world in the likeness of human flesh to save us from our sin. Jesus took on Himself the sin of all mankind.

> **God made him who had no sin to be sin for us, so that in him we might become the righteousness of God.**
> **(2 Corinthians 5:21)**

> **For it is by grace you have been saved, through faith—and this is not from yourselves, it is the gift of God—not by works, so that no one can boast.**
> **(Ephesians 2:8–9)**

Accepting His free gift is the only way we can be saved and remove the blockage of sin so His forgiveness can flow through us and His truth and love can heal our brokenness of mind and body.

> **To the Jews who had believed him, Jesus said, "If you hold to my teaching, you are really my disciples. Then you will know the truth, and the truth will set you free."**
> **(John 8:31–32)**

The Jabez Prayer

Jabez cried out to the God of Israel, "Oh, that you would bless me and enlarge my territory! Let your hand be with me, and keep me free harm so that I will be free from pain." And God granted his request.
(1 Chronicles 4:10)

Some would say it sounds very selfish to ask God to bless and enlarge your territory. Before we can make a judgment on a prayer like this, the big question is, why did he ask this from God, and what kind of blessing was Jabez asking for? Was he selfishly asking to be blessed with material possessions and land for his own benefit? Did he want his territory enlarged out of pride so he'd finally get some respect and admiration from his family and contemporaries? We know very little about Jabez, except what is stated in the preceding verse:

Jabez was more honorable than his brothers. His mother had named him Jabez saying, "I gave birth to him in pain."
(1 Chronicles 4:9)

This doesn't tell us very much other than the fact he had brothers, and he was evidently more honorable than they were, and his mother named him Jabez because of the pain he caused her at childbirth. I can only imagine what it would have been like to be constantly reminded that I had caused my mother great pain being born. Especially, since I had absolutely no control over my own birth.

It would've made me feel guilty every time she even looked at me, and it would've been even worse if I had siblings who made it their business to constantly remind me of this and put me down. The Bible didn't say his brothers did that, but it doesn't require much imagination to jump to that conclusion since they apparently weren't very honorable men.

A person like Jabez could have been shaped by this dilemma in one of two ways. The person could've either turned into a very hardhearted, angry, hateful person, or a very tenderhearted, sensitive, and caring person. Evidently, Jabez became the latter. The Bible said he was "more honorable" than his brothers. There are a few other keys to understanding the attitude of Jabez's heart in his prayer. They can be found in the second portion of his request:

> **Let your hand be with me, and keep me from harm, so that I will be free from pain.**

- He asked God's hand to be with him. That kind of request doesn't come from a hardened heart. It comes from a heart that loves and honors God.
- He asked God to keep him from harm. That kind of request doesn't come from an angry, vengeful heart, either. It comes from a sensitive heart that trusts God.
- He asked God that he be kept from pain. That kind of request doesn't come from an unfeeling heart. It comes from a tender, caring heart that no longer wants to be a recipient of pain or a cause of pain to others.

God saw into the tender heart of Jabez and what He saw greatly pleased Him. God knew that the blessings Jabez was requesting weren't asked in selfishness. He knew He could trust him with them. He knew Jabez wouldn't abuse or misuse these blessings because Jabez's character had already been tested by trouble and tribulations in his life, and he passed the test with flying colors.

Based on his proven character, I believe Jabez's request to be blessed and to have his territory enlarged were of a pure motive. Jabez had a heart for God and wanted more than anything else to be blessed with more of God's presence in his life. I imagine he had it in his heart to become prosperous enough to be a big blessing to his mother in repayment for all the pain she suffered bringing him into the world. I also imagine the enlargement of his territory being used to influence many others for good, drawing them closer to God. And he probably gave God glory by telling everyone his testimony and letting them know all his blessings came from Him. I believe Jabez wanted to be blessed so he could be a blessing. "So God granted his request."

There are many lessons we can learn from Jabez and this short prayer:

- Some difficulties in life, we are born into and have no control over. Unsolicited troubles and offenses experienced in life can be used by God as a testing ground. With that in mind, we must take full responsibility for how we allow troubles to shape us.
- A humble and surrendered heart is the best way to prepare for a future full of God's abundant blessings.
- God is very generous and is not offended by big requests.
- It's God's will to bless us and enlarge our territory when our lives are pleasing to Him.
- God wants us to ask for His hand to be with us, so it's wise to ask God for His protection.
- A truly wise person asks God for His protection

This brief prayer by Jabez can become a model for us, but we can have even more confidence in prayer than he did, because we are under the new covenant. Jesus has promised us answers to our prayers when we ask for anything in His name that is according to His will.

Based on what we learned from Jabez's prayer, it would be wise to examine our hearts and know our motives before we offer a prayer like his. We should honestly ask ourselves these questions:

- Do I believe first of all that it is God's will to bless me because I am in Christ?
- Is my heart grounded enough in Him to handle an abundant outpouring of His blessings?
- Am I asking Him to bless me so that I can be a blessing to others?
- If God enlarges my territory, will I use any new power and influence to benefit His kingdom?

If we can answer "Yes, Lord" to these questions, we can be assured what we ask is according to His will. Then, we can wait with confident expectation, knowing we will get the same results Jabez did.

"So God granted his request."

Paul's Prayer for the Ephesians

One of my favorite prayers in the whole Bible is found in the third chapter of Ephesians. It is one of many prayers the apostle Paul prayed for the Gentile churches he founded. It begins with him explaining his calling as the apostle to the Gentiles. His assignment was to reveal the mystery of Christ, which had been hidden in ages past, but was then being made known to the rulers and authorities in the heavenly realms.

He reassured the Ephesians that through faith in Christ, they could approach God with freedom and confidence. He said they were not to be discouraged by His sufferings for them, because it was for their glory. This prayer so blessed me when I discovered it that I committed it to memory several years ago. I have prayed it more times than I can count, but never in a way of repetitive religious ritual.

I pray this prayer in the power of the Spirit, personalized with the name of the person I am praying for imposed into it, or I put it in first person for myself. It condenses an enormous amount of truth about our blessings in Christ and is a prayer of supplication for power!

> **For this reason I kneel before the Father, from whom every family in heaven and on earth derives its name. I pray that out of his glorious riches he may strengthen you with power through his Spirit in your inner being, so that Christ may dwell in your hearts through faith. And I pray that you, being rooted and established in love, may have power, together with all the Lord's holy people, to grasp how wide and long and high and deep is the love of Christ, and to know this love that surpasses knowledge—that you may be filled to the measure of all the fullness of God.**
>
> **Now to him who is able to do immeasurably more than all we ask or imagine, according to his power that is at work within us, to him be glory in the church and in Christ Jesus throughout all generations, forever and ever! Amen.**
> **(Ephesians 3:14–21)**

- The prayer begins with worship, recognizing God as our Abba, Father.
- We are His family. He named us and knows us by name.
- He strengthens us out of His glorious riches and there is no limit to His glory.

- He gives us might through His indwelling Holy Spirit so that Christ can dwell in our hearts through faith.
- His love roots and established us, giving us power.

The power of love unites the church and enables us to grasp the all-encompassing nature of Christ's love, which fills the universe in all directions.

- His love surpasses knowledge.
- His love fills us up with God's fullness.
- He is able to do immeasurably more than we can ask or imagine.
- His blessings and outpour of goodness is according to His power at work in us.
- He deserves all the glory in the church and in Christ Jesus.
- His glory is throughout all generations for eternity.

So be it!

The Believers Prayer for Boldness

During the days of the early church, Peter performed a miraculous sign by healing a man lame from birth. They preached the name of Jesus and five thousand were saved. When those in authority heard of it, they arrested Peter and John, interrogated them, and commanded them to not teach or speak any more in the name of Jesus, but Peter and John responded to them:

> **Which is right in God's eye: to listen to you, or to him?**
> **(Acts 4:19)**

They could find no way to punish Peter and John, because the people glorified God so much for the miraculous healing. So, the rulers had to let them go. When Peter and John returned to the other believers, they told them all that had taken place and what the chief priests and elders had said to them.

> **When they heard this, they raised their voices together in prayer to God. "Sovereign Lord," they said, "you made the heavens and the earth and the sea, and everything in them. You spoke by the Holy Spirit through the mouth of your servant, our father David:**
>
> > **'Why do the nations rage and the people plot in vain? The kings of the earth rise up and the rulers band together against the Lord and against his anointed one.'**
>
> **Indeed Herod and Pontius Pilate met together with the Gentiles and the people of Israel in this city to conspire against your holy servant Jesus, whom you anointed. They did what your power and will had decided beforehand should happen. Now, Lord, consider their threats and enable your servants to speak your word with great boldness. Stretch out your hand to heal and perform signs and wonders through the name of your holy servant Jesus."**
>
> **After they prayed, the place where they were meeting was shaken. And they were all filled with the Holy Spirit and spoke the word of God boldly.**
>
> **(Acts 4:24–31)**

When we go into the world to preach the good news of Jesus, we will encounter opposition. Although the United States was founded on Christian principles, in recent years, the freedom to share our faith has been under attack. It is being gradually stripped away by the courts, which repeatedly use the phrase, "Separation of church and state," as justification to deny religious freedom instead of enforcing the First Amendment's intent to protect the free exercise of it.

The so-called "wall of separation" is evidently not high enough to prevent some states from trying to use new laws to require churches to perform certain ceremonies that violate our biblical principles. If possible, enemies of the gospel would abuse governmental power until they could silence the sharing of the Christian message on the streets, and even dictate to us what we can and cannot preach within the walls of our own churches.

They are persistent in their efforts to get our country's official motto, "In God We Trust," removed from our currency. Outspoken preachers of God's Word are being identified and labeled by them as purveyors of "hate speech." The developing message to Christians from the anti-Christ powers of our day resembles the one given to Peter and John by the Sanhedrin.

**Not to speak or teach at all in the name of Jesus.
Acts 4:18**

The Devil knows his time is short, so his hostility and attacks on the gospel of Christ is accelerating very quickly. We still have a degree of free speech here to proclaim our faith in Christ, but there are many places around the world where Christians are dying every day for standing by their faith and refusing to deny Jesus. We are living in the last days, and the Bible warns us, a time is coming when the powers of darkness working through the governments will force people to choose between faith in Christ or death. As the end-time church, we must take to heart what Jesus said to His first followers as also applying to us.

**I tell you, whoever publicly acknowledges
me before others, the Son of Man will also**

acknowledge before the angels of God. But whoever disowns me before others will be disowned before the angels of God.
(Luke 12:8–9)

When you are brought before synagogues, rulers and authorities, do not worry about how you will defend yourself or what you will say, for the Holy Spirit will teach you at that time what you should say.
(Luke 12:11–12)

Our response to their pressure to censor our speech should be the same as Peter and John's:

But Peter and John replied, "Which is right in God's eyes: to listen to you, or to him? You be the judges! As for us, we cannot help speaking about what we have seen and heard."
(Acts 4:19–20)

And as the apostle Paul asked the Ephesians to pray and ask the Spirit to give him boldness in Ephesians 6:19, so must we.

Prayer

Ask the Lord in your own words to give the twenty-first-century church boldness and power to carry the gospel to the world. Ask Him to seal the truths you just learned in your heart and to give you boldness by the Spirit to stand for Jesus no matter what the cost.

CHAPTER 8

Praying in the Name of Jesus

Recently, I've overheard a discussion in Christian circles on whether prayer should be offered to the Father in Jesus' name, or if it's also permissible to offer prayer directly to Jesus. The fact that this discussion has escalated into an actual debate amazes me! There's a prominent line being drawn in the sand with Christians on both sides, angrily waving their fists at each other.

When you look in the Bible to consider the merits for the arguments being used, it becomes quite apparent, at least to me, this is a bit of a silly debate. Let me explain what I mean. First, if you would think this is a Trinitarian versus non-Trinitarian disagreement, it isn't. Interestingly, there are Trinitarians on both sides of the issue! As we look at this, I think we first have to remind ourselves:

- Prayer is: a spiritual conversation with God.
- Prayer isn't: a religious ritual.

Okay, now with that in mind, let's move forward. I'm not foolish or naive enough to try and explain the Trinity, but perhaps we can agree on some of its characteristics. Trinitarians believe God exists in three personalities, parts, or facets: Father, Son, and Holy Spirit. He's one God, whose three persons are each distinct, yet of one essence. All three are God. For the sake of this discussion on who we can pray to, here are some Scriptures to support the deity of the second person of the Trinity, Christ.

> **In the beginning was the Word, and the Word was with God, and the Word was God.**
> **(John 1:1)**

> **Moreover, the Father judges no one, but has entrusted all judgment to the Son, that all may honor the Son just as they honor the Father. Whoever does not honor the Son does not honor the Father who sent Him.**
> **(John 5:22–23)**

Jesus told those who were questioning His identity,

> **I and the Father are one.**
> **(John 10:30)**

> **"Very truly I tell you," Jesus answered, "before Abraham was born, I am!"**
> **(John 8:58)**

> **Jesus answered: "Don't you know me, Philip, even after I have been among you such a long time? Anyone who has seen me has seen the Father. How can you say, "Show us the Father"?**
> **(John 14:9)**

Jesus affirmed His deity and authority to His disciples.

> **And I will do whatever you ask in my name, so that the Father may be glorified in the Son. You**

> **may ask me for anything in my name, and I will do it.**
> **(John 14:13–14)**

> **If you remain in me and my words remain in you, ask whatever you wish, and it will be done for you.**
> **(John 15:7)**

> **Then Jesus came to them and said, "All authority in heaven and on earth has been given to me. Therefore go and make disciples of all nations, baptizing them in the name of the Father and of the Son and of the Holy Spirit.**
> **(Matthew 28:18–19)**

We learn from these Scriptures that Jesus and the Father are one. Jesus said He did what He saw the Father do and only said what He heard Him say. He was always doing God's work and God's will. He followed this path completely for all three years of His earthly ministry and it didn't change. Everything He did on earth was in the Father's name because He sent Him on an assignment. Jesus said He has been given all authority *in heaven* and on earth. Wouldn't that reasonably include the authority in heaven to receive and answer prayers?

Jesus gave His disciples a special prayer in Matthew 6 that can help us figure this out. He told them to pray, "Our Father in heaven." Okay! I realize He said, "Our Father," and I'm not backing away from that. It's perfectly clear that in everything Jesus did and said, He always gave honor to His Father and never Himself. He didn't need to seek His own honor because His Father always honored Him: "Your kingdom come, your will be done on earth as it is in heaven."

What is going on in heaven with the Father's will is what He wants to be going on in the earth. This carries over to Jesus as well. Their will is as much in agreement now as it was when They created the universe together. They were, are, and always have been in perfect harmony because They share the same essence, God.

God's throne is the place of authority and power, and the Bible tells us Jesus is seated right there, right now, at His Father's side. It may seem like I am leaning toward what some know as a Jesus-Only doctrine. It rejects the concept of the Trinity and teaches Jesus is the Father, the Son, and the Holy Spirit. As I already said, I am a Trinitarian! My answer to the Jesus-Only crowd is a trinity of "No! No! No!"

And no way am I trying to imply the concept of the Godhead is easy to comprehend. God is so beyond our human intellect, it's a miracle we can have any kind of relationship with Him. The relationship between Father and Son is hard to understand, so it's no wonder we have so much trouble trying to grasp it. We may grapple with it, but Jesus never did. As we saw before, when asked if He was the Messiah, Jesus told them, "I and the Father are one." Inspired by the Holy Spirit, the apostle Paul wrote the following when speaking of Christ:

> **Who being in very nature God, did not consider equality with God something to be used to his own advantage, rather, he made himself nothing by taking the very nature of a servant, being made in human likeness.**
> **(Philippians 2:6–7)**

There is no competition, no conflict, no distance between Father and Son. They are in perfect sync. I don't know why we find that so difficult to understand and feel the need to make their relationship into a competition that glorifies one at the expense of the other. Jesus explains what being one with the Father means.

> **Very truly I tell you, the Son can do nothing by himself; he can only do what he sees his Father doing, because whatever the Father does the Son also does.**
> **(John 5:19)**

They have been one from eternity past to eternity future. This did not change when Jesus stepped out of heaven into time to fulfill the Father's will on earth. When He completed His assignment of sacrificing Himself for us, He went back to the Father and took His seat at the Father's right hand on His majestic throne of power and authority. From there He is interceding for us according to Romans 8:34. This will not change at the end of time when they return to perfect oneness.

> **Then the end will come, when he hands over the kingdom to God the Father after he has destroyed all dominion, authority and power. For he must reign until he has put all enemies under his feet. The last enemy to be destroyed is death. For "he has put everything under his feet." Now when it says that "everything" has been put under him, it is clear that this does not include God himself, who put everything under Christ. When he has done this, then the Son himself will be made subject to him who put everything under him, so that God may be all in all.**
> **(1 Corinthians 15:24–28)**

Every prayer offered in the Spirit and in truth rises to the throne of grace where both the Father and the Son sit together in one essence, in perfect unity. They receive our prayers in that unity of oneness. Can you imagine a dispute between them when the

Pharisees were stoning Steven to death and he prayed: **"Lord Jesus, receive my spirit."**? (Acts 7:59).

Do you think Jesus looked over at the Father and said, "Oops! Sorry, Abba, we can't answer that one because he didn't present that prayer right."?

Enough on that; let's move on to consider the phrase, "in the name of" by examining the following two examples:

Let's look at it first in the natural realm. An officer of the law is on patrol. He confronts someone breaking the law with violent disorderly conduct that is endangering the safety of others.

- The officer takes authority to restore peace by giving a firm command, "Cease, in the name of the law!
- The officer speaks in confidence, knowing his or her authority to bring order is official. The officer knows the command was backed up by the power of the agency that delegated that authority to him or her.
- The offender knows yielding to the officer's authority to enforce the law is mandatory. Resisting the officer's command is not optional.

Now let's flip it to the spiritual realm. A Christian doing ministry confronts spiritual darkness that is actively breaking the peace and endangering the spiritual well being of others.

- The Christian takes authority over the situation, demanding peace to be restored by giving a firm command to the disrupting spirit, "Cease, in the name of Jesus." Now, let's examine this action more closely:
- The Christian speaks in confidence, knowing his or her authority to bring order is official. This Christian knows the command was backed by the power of Christ who delegated that authority to him or her.

- The offending dark force knows yielding to the Christian's authority in Jesus' name is mandatory. Resisting the name of Jesus is not optional.

This brings to mind the Scripture found in Acts when Paul cast a spirit of divination out of an irritating fortune teller who was following them around:

> **She kept this up for many days. Finally Paul became so annoyed that he turned around and said to the spirit, "In the name of Jesus Christ I command you to come out of her!" At that moment the spirit left her.**
> **(Acts 16:18)**

Here are some additional "in my name" Scriptures spoken by Jesus:

> **For where two or three gather *in my name*, there am I with them.**
> **(Matthew 18:20, *emphasis added*)**

> **You did not choose me, but I chose you and appointed you so that you might go and bear fruit—fruit that will last—and so that whatever you ask *in my name* the Father will give you.**
> **(John 15:16, *emphasis added*)**

> **Until now you have not asked for anything *in my name*. Ask and you will receive, and your joy will be complete.**
> **(John 16:24, *emphasis added*)**

This was in one of the Pauline letters:

> **And whatever you do, whether in word or deed,**
> **do it all *in the name* of the Lord Jesus, giving**
> **thanks to God the Father through him.**
> **(Colossians 3:17, *emphasis added*).**

Before Jesus returned to the Father, He gave the church a commission to fulfill in His name:

> **and repentance for the forgiveness of sins will be**
> **preached *in his name* to all nations, beginning**
> **at Jerusalem.**
> **(Luke 24:47, *emphasis added*).**

The work of the kingdom is done for the benefit of the King. "In His name" means the work is being done in His power and by His authority. We are ambassadors for Christ sent into the entire world with the message of reconciliation.

> **Therefore, if anyone is in Christ, the new**
> **creation has come. The old has gone, the new is**
> **here! All this is from God, who reconciled us to**
> **himself through Christ and gave us the ministry**
> **of reconciliation: that God was reconciling the**
> **world to himself in Christ, not counting people's**
> **sins against them. And he has committed to us**
> **the message of reconciliation. We are therefore**
> **Christ's ambassadors, as though God were**
> **making his appeal through us. We implore you**
> **on Christ's behalf: Be reconciled to God.**
> **(2 Corinthians 5:17–20)**

With these Scriptures before us, we can see things more clearly from God's perspective. We can go in confidence, knowing Jesus didn't give us His name to use like an incantation or some secret password to get us through heaven's doors. When we pray to God, we are addressing Him in all His essence. Approaching the Father in prayer in Jesus' name is not a formal act of separation of powers. He didn't give us His name so the Father will hear our prayers and answer them.

"In His name" is a verbal acknowledgment of our status of being *in Christ*. It is not for the Father's benefit; it is for ours. By this, we can have full confidence in approaching God's throne. Jesus promised whatever we ask for in His name, He would do it. From our position in Him, we can ask for help and strength to do His will on the earth as it is in heaven and power to endure temptations.

When we are functioning in His name, we're acting in the role of an ambassador for the kingdom of God on official assignment. Saying, "in the name of Jesus" is like flashing our badge to let the principalities and powers in the heavenly realm and on earth know that His authority and the power of His Spirit have been given to get His will done.

Whenever we do the will of God, we will encounter opposition from the Devil. During those times, we must stand on the Word of God, reminding the Devil that we have authority in Christ to do the work of the kingdom on this earth. When we resist the Devil, God's Word says, he will flee. He has no other choice. The authority of God's Word and the name of Jesus have power, and the realm of darkness knows this.

Whenever we speak God's Word in faith, it is as if God Himself were speaking, "making His appeal through us." When we speak the name of Jesus with authority, there is power for deliverance and healing! We in the body of Christ must know God's Word to confidently use His name. He has called us to accomplish mighty works for His glory.

It is important that we remember, using Jesus' name when we pray is not a formality or ritualistic way to end a prayer. When we pray, we are communicating with God in His Trinitarian essence. Praying in Jesus' name is communion with the Father; knowing we are in the Son, with access through the indwelling Holy Spirit! Prayer to God is experiencing God in all His fullness.

Prayer

Triune God, Father, Son, and Holy Spirit, I am so thankful that You live in me. Help me to realize that prayer in its purest form is abiding in You. ["Abiding in You" and "praying without ceasing" mean the same thing.] Help me to grow in this truth so that I can walk in confidence and remain constantly aware of Your holy presence both in me and around me in power to do Your will. I am more than a conqueror because in my weakness, Your power is being perfected. I know that I am never alone. Amen.

PART THREE

Breaking Through in Prayer

CHAPTER 9

When You Have Trouble Praying

E ven when we have a good understanding of prayer, there will be times we'll have trouble praying. It doesn't mean God is ignoring us because He's angry with us. It may just mean we need to connect with Him in a different way sometimes. Let me explain it this way:

I'm a night person not a morning person! It seems like I don't even shift into second gear until everyone else has gone down for the night (my husband's version of going to bed). In the last few years, I changed from working a nine-to-five corporate job to self-employment. Somehow, I've reprogrammed myself to stay up very, very late, but I didn't do it on purpose. It's gotten to the point now that I don't even feel like my day is over until the minute hand of the bedroom wall clock passes the halfway mark between 2 and 3 a.m. I need about five hours of sleep, so if you do the math, you will see I'm not much of an early riser.

I like my conversation with God to be the very last thing I do before sleeping and the first thing I do upon awaking. What some might consider their early morning prayer at 3 a.m., I consider my late-night prayer. I am deep into the realm of the Spirit, communing with the Lord in devotions, when most others are out and in the process of their workday.

My unconventional sleeping pattern has also changed the way I do many other things. I own and operate a resale store, so as the boss, I get to decide my hours based on my preference. Needless to say, being open from noon to 7 p.m. was my choice. It irritates morning shoppers, but works great for afternoon shoppers, and it works for me. Besides, I'm most energetic, productive, and creative between noon and midnight.

On my Sunday off day, I go to church, then occasionally share a leisurely lunch with friends, afterwards. Sundays after church and lunch, I also like to do my weekly grocery shopping. Believe it or not, I really love grocery shopping. I not only find it a good way to get a little exercise, it's also very relaxing. It's fun shopping around for bargains. It's my habit to frequent several different stores to make sure I score all the best weekend deals. When I've finished my shopping routine, I return to the house to cook a nice Sunday dinner before I settle down and hopefully get a little nap.

One particular Sunday, instead of napping, my intention was to do some writing on this book. But I couldn't seem to get myself focused enough to get into it. After watching a couple of programs on Christian TV, I discovered I wasn't in a writing mood. Instead of staying up really late like I usually do, I decided to begin my nighttime devotions with the Lord earlier than usual and go to sleep around midnight for a change.

I set my alarm a few hours earlier than usual so I could jump-start my day with a nice, long devotional time and still have time to do some writing before I headed off to the store. My nightly conversation with the Lord began at 10:30 p.m. I barely got going, then I drifted off, fast to sleep, midsentence.

Monday morning I awakened a half hour before the alarm went off. Even though I had a lot more sleep than usual, rousing myself to full alertness was difficult. I got up, washed my face, and turned on my reading lamp. No matter what I did, I couldn't seem to get it together. I asked the Holy Spirit to fill me up so I could worship my way into the Lord's presence, but I couldn't focus my spirit.

Since I was having trouble praying, I picked up the Bible, thinking that maybe I could enter His presence on the wings of truth. Even reading the Psalms couldn't get me out of my drowsy distracted state, into the realm of the Spirit.

My struggle of drifting in and out of alertness continued for two hours with absolutely no spiritual progress. There was no more time left for prayer or writing. I had to start getting ready for my day at the store.

As usual, I chitchat with the Lord as I drive to the store. I told Him how much I loved Him and how much I regretted missing spending time with Him that morning. When I got to the store, I felt off balance the first few hours. The customer traffic was low in the store. I couldn't seem to decide whether I should focus my downtime to work on unfinished sewing projects, redress my window mannequins, or catch up on my writing.

I felt very uneasy and was still having trouble focusing. For the life of me, I couldn't put my finger on what my problem was. After a cup of coffee, I decided I didn't feel much like trying to coordinate six new outfits for the mannequins. The thought of sewing or writing didn't appeal to me either. All these activities required creativity, and I wasn't feeling the least bit creative. I seriously thought about closing the store, returning home, and getting back in bed, but I knew that would be counterproductive. It might feel good, but it would be a total waste of time.

Since the coffee didn't kick me into gear, I drank a half can of energy drink. When the caffeine combination finally started to kick in, I decided the best thing would be to engage my body in some strenuous physical activity until my creative juices started to flow. Maybe working up a sweat sweeping the floor would direct some creative energy through my veins into my mind.

I grabbed the broom and began very enthusiastically sweeping the carpet and moving clothes racks around. As I was sweeping, I wondered if the uneasiness I felt was a warning that something unusual was going to happen that day. I thought about my kids and husband. I wondered if one of them was going through something and needed me.

As if in response to my thoughts, I heard a still small voice whisper in my spiritual ear, "Tongues. You need to pray in your prayer language." I hesitated for a second. I was a bit startled by the clarity of what I heard, then thought, "Hmm, that's a great idea!" I immediately and quietly prayed in tongues, just above a whisper as I continued aggressively sweeping.

Within seconds, I felt a clear sense of release. The heavy uneasiness lifted, and the peace of God flooded my being. The Holy Spirit had been talking to me a lot since I obeyed His instruction to do this writing assignment. The message I heard that day was as loud and clear as anything He had said so far. What I had experienced wasn't coincidental; it had a purpose. He used life circumstances to tell me the next topic I was to write about. When I finished sweeping, I went directly over to my computer, brought up the document and began typing, "When you have trouble praying," and the words began to flow and my creative block melted away like an ice-cream cone on a hot summer day.

It's pretty much common knowledge that writers from time to time struggle with writer's block. It's extremely frustrating. Suddenly everything comes to a stop right in the middle of a piece you're working on. It happens quickly. Without warning or any apparent reason, focus is lost and creativity stops flowing. They want to write—even need to write—but a decent sentence won't come together.

The harder the effort, the worse writing paralysis gets. I have no idea what causes this. I can't imagine any writer wanting this experience, but from what I've heard, even the best writer goes through it to some extent, sooner or later. I'm not sure what writers do to break through this block. Needless to say, it requires a creative imagination to break through a creative block. Different things work for different people, depending on how they are wired.

I think there are times when Christians experience something very similar to a writer's block. I'll call it a "prayer's block." It's extremely frustrating to want to pray or even need to pray, but for some unknown reason to have trouble praying. That was exactly how I felt. I experienced prayer paralysis! That is disconcerting especially when you're in the middle of writing a book about prayer!

I expect I am not the only Christian to experience an episode of "prayer's block." As a matter of fact, I believe that's why the Holy Spirit walked me through an episode of it. It made it personal so I could write about it from an empathetic point of view. I had every intention to put a section in the book about praying in tongues but kept putting it off. I wasn't sure exactly how to approach the topic. It's a topic that can be very divisive if not handled with great sensitivity. Fortunately, the Holy Spirit knew exactly what was needed to get praying in tongues rolling.

The body of Christ isn't in agreement about the subject of tongues. It is a tricky discussion in mixed denominational circles because of differing opinions and very strong feelings one way or the other. Discussions can become very heated and contentious. Christians I've talked to usually fall into one of four basic groups or schools of thought:

1. Absolutely *no*
2. Absolutely *yes*
3. Extremely *yes*
4. Sometimes *yes*, sometimes *no* (conditional tongues)

Group 1 says tongues of any type, along with all the supernatural gifts spoken about in the Bible, ended with the completion of the New Testament Canon. From their perspective, when the full Bible was completed, supernatural gifts were no longer necessary. These gifts had their purpose, but it's over now. They perceive people claiming to speak in tongues as self-deceived. They only babble gibberish and follow it up with imagined interpretations. Some will go so far as to suggest speaking in tongues could be an exposure to demonic influence.

Group 2 says all the supernatural gifts have continued uninterrupted since the Holy Spirit fell on the first-century church in the upper room on the day of Pentecost. They allow prophetic tongues, (preferably with interpretation), in their services. They also permit unrestricted prayer tongues, (with discretion). The prerequisite for expression of both is that they be done decently and in order.

Group 3, similar to 2, allows prophetic and prayer tongues, (usually with no restrictions). Their services may seem a bit too free flowing to some Christians and even chaotic to others. Another difference between groups 2 and 3 is that some in group 3 teach that speaking in tongues is the only undeniable evidence of the baptism of the Holy Spirit. As far as they are concerned, if you don't speak in tongues, you haven't yet experienced the baptism of the Holy Spirit. They aren't saying you're not saved, just that you haven't been baptized with the power of the Holy Ghost.

Group 4 says the gifts are for today but in practice, they don't encourage speaking in tongues during regular services. They don't outright forbid them either, but consider uncontrolled, impromptu speaking in tongues as overly disruptive to the service. Besides that, there's a concern that a sudden outburst of tongues would scare newcomers off. Regular church attendees hold to an unspoken church rule of etiquette when it comes to tongues. During service, it's best to keep firm control over your gifts and limit tongue talking to your personal prayer closet.

I've even heard there are some churches in this group that require a person to approach a deacon beforehand and ask for permission to speak a message in tongues, if they want to share it with the congregation. If this is approved, they are ushered to the microphone at an appropriate time to share it with the congregation.

Personally, I'd say my understanding of tongues falls closer to group 2. However, I admit that although I have the gift of prophetic tongues and interpretation, it has been a very long time since I've done it during a service. The church I attend and most of those I've recently visited lean more toward the group 3 approach. I definitely don't want to be considered disruptive or out of order during a service. I practice my prayer language often in my personal prayer closet, when alone in my car, or in a whisper during worship services so no one will hear me. Until the Spirit tells me otherwise, tongues are between God and me.

The Holy Spirit gives spiritual gifts according to His foreknowledge. The Bible says, **"For God's gifts and his call are irrevocable." (Romans 11:29)** Some may take issue with anyone intentionally refraining to use a gift. I understand their point, but I haven't read anywhere in the Bible that He takes away free will when He assigns them.

I'd also like to note that tongues are not normally something that takes over to such a degree that self-control is lost. A believer with a gift of preaching, healing, prophecy, tongues, or any other gift can choose how and when to use a gift or even not to use it, at all. The Holy Spirit gives the anointing to use it, but the recipient must consciously yield to Him in order for the gift to powerfully flow through them in ministry.

Please don't misunderstand what I'm saying. Although free will permits choice on how and when to use a gift, every believer will be held accountable to Christ for their choices on how their gift was used or not used. We will be unable to give any excuse for misusing or under using our gifts when we stand before the judgment seat of Christ. It is much like Jesus' parable of the accounting of the coins in Luke 19:11–28. Our gifts were given with the expectation they'd be used in ministry to others for the purpose of multiplying the kingdom. If a believer chooses to bury their gift(s) in a hole, there will be stern consequences.

Prayer tongues are one of the wonderful benefits of being filled with the Holy Spirit. The human spirit can be communicating with

Christ even when the body and the mind are occupied with other tasks. I like the attitude Paul had:

> **I thank God that I speak in tongues more than all of you. But in the church I would rather speak five intelligible words to instruct others than ten thousand words in a tongue.**
> **(1 Corinthians 14:18–19)**

> **For anyone who speaks in a tongue does not speak to people but to God. Indeed, no one understands them; they utter mysteries by the Spirit.**
> **(1 Corinthians 14:2)**

Verse 4 goes on to say, the person **"edifies themselves."** This means the spirit is being built up or strengthened by praying in tongues. Something is happening in the inner being on a level much deeper than human intellect can possibly grasp:

> **For if I pray in a tongue, my spirit prays, but my mind is unfruitful.**
> **(1 Corinthians 14:14).**

Have you ever experienced a general uneasiness around you when you entered a room? You couldn't put your finger on what was wrong, but somehow you knew, whatever it was, it wasn't from the kingdom of light. It is often a general feeling of unease, irritability and heaviness like I shared I was experiencing. In those times, it may be due to the acceleration of demonic activity in an area. When that happens, a stronghold of some type is either present or being built up.

I can often sense it when I enter an area with this kind of activity present. The Spirit has not yet given me the level of discerning of spirits to distinguish what kind of principality or stronghold agenda is active. I can just spiritually discern their presence. Even if I don't know their specific agenda, I do know that it intends to hinder the will of God and prevent the Word from reaching those who need the truth.

Praying in tongues is very powerful as a weapon in the spiritual realm. It is how I deal with things my mind can't fully grasp. It helps me develop clarity and the sensitivity needed to discern an ambient spiritual environment of darkness around me. Dark spirits dispel confusion in an attempt to adversely affect my ability to hear from God. The Holy Spirit in me sets off an alarm alerting me to the stronghold activity of a principality or power in the spiritual realm.

Praying in tongues, in the power of the Spirit, repels the cloak of darkness they are attempting to surround me with. It delivers me from their attack, enabling me to clearly hear from the Spirit which applicable truth from God's Word will be the most effective weapon to use against them. Speaking His Word out loud pulls down strongholds and restores peace and order.

Some try to put prayer tongues and prophetic tongues in the same category, but they are two different applications. One is intended to benefit self; the other benefits the body of Christ. Paul says in verse 13, **"For this reason the one who speaks in a tongue should pray that they may interpret what they say."** Notice the words "speaks" and "say." This is referring to speaking prophetic tongues aloud in the presence of others or in church services. It continues,

> **So what shall I do? I will pray with my spirit, but I will also pray with my understanding; I will sing with my spirit, but I will also sing with my understanding.**
> **(1 Corinthians 14:15)**

He explains in the next verse, that understanding makes it possible for others present to also benefit from the truth and be able to say "amen."

According to Paul, when there is no interpretation, it is more beneficial to speak intelligible words in the presence of others so they can understand and be edified, than to pray aloud in an unknown language, which only edifies self. When in the presence of God, alone, with no other person listening, it is a totally different thing. Praying in tongues uplifts and strengthens the spirit with power. The spirit knows so much more than the mind because human minds cannot discern the things of the spirit realm. Those who build themselves up by praying in the spirit and studying the Word of God are more spiritually prepared to hear and obey the Holy Spirit.

Of course, the body, soul, and spirit must cooperate together to live a balanced life, but the key to power in the realm of the spirit is learning how to walk in the spirit. Walking in the spirit is living under the control of the Holy Spirit who abides in us. When the whole being is under His control, it is what is known as being "filled with the Spirit." That is when a believer is under such a powerful anointing that the Holy Spirit is free to work through them to perform signs and wonders. It is the spirit man that has the mind of Christ, because that is where Christ lives.

Real power is found in bringing the whole being, spirit, mind/soul, and body under submission to the Spirit of God. I like to think of my human spirit as the control central of my spirit being. It is counterproductive to try to emotionally work up something in the spirit. Being led by the Spirit is an act of God's grace working and willing in us to do His pleasure. Our job is to surrender to Him by dying to self-will and self-effort, to let God's will take full control.

> **Therefore, I urge you brothers and sisters, in view of God's mercy, to offer your bodies as a living sacrifice, holy and pleasing to God—this is your true and proper worship.**
> **(Romans 12:1)**

Only by submitting to God can we learn to effectively use the mighty weapons of the Spirit. We must never forget that we are in a battle of light against darkness, and the weapon of praying in tongues is one of our most powerful weapons. Many resist this. They think speaking in tongues is being *out of control,* and they constantly struggle to stay *in control.* They want to have complete understanding of everything that is going on, but we don't need to understand everything to be a good warrior for God.

There are times it is better if we just trust Him and not try so hard to understand. Sometimes, our most difficult battle is internal because of a tendency of leaning to our understanding instead of trusting the Lord in all our ways and acknowledging Him. That is what the walk of faith is all about: trusting and leaning on the power of the Spirit to do what we cannot do.

God has given Him to us to help us in our human weaknesses. Praying in tongues helps with this internal battle in a way that transcends human understanding. Pray in tongues when you don't know how or what to pray for. When you do, the Spirit intercedes according to God's will and in His time, discernment and revelation of His will is given to us.

Prayer

Now speak to God in your heavenly prayer language. If you have never done this before, ask the Spirit to help you, and you shall receive it. It is not something another can teach you by telling you to mimic their sounds. It is Spirit taught. Set your spirit free and open yourself to His guidance. Don't worry about how you sound. It is your spiritual language and God is revealing secrets to your spirit.

CHAPTER 10

The Power of Praying in Confidence

> This is the confidence we have in approaching
> God: that if we ask anything according to his
> will, he hears us. And if we know he hears us—
> whatever we ask—we know that we have what
> we asked of Him.
> (1 John 5:14–15)

Learning how to approach God in confidence is an important ingredient in revolutionizing our prayer life. Jesus promised we could have this confidence in the above verse, so let's break these two verses down and look very closely at what they can teach us about praying in this way.

"This Is the Confidence"

Confidence means assurance and certainty! It means having faith as we approach God, believing in His faithfulness and ability to do what He says in His Word He will do. But how do we get this kind of faith?

> **Consequently, faith comes from hearing the**
> **message, and the message is heard through the**
> **word about Christ.**
> **(Romans 10:17)**

The very ability to know anything spiritual comes from the Holy Spirit. We come into this world spiritually blind. At the moment anyone hears the gospel, the Holy Spirit has to remove the spiritual blinders placed there by the Devil before they can even see Christ's glory, making it possible to respond in faith and believe unto salvation.

> **If you declare with your mouth, "Jesus is Lord,"**
> **and believe in your heart that God raised him**
> **from the dead, you will be saved.**
> **(Romans 10:9)**

The person who sincerely confesses and believes in Christ is instantly born again. From that moment forward, he or she can be confident of his or her salvation. God said it in His Word, and He keeps all of His promises, so there should be no doubt. Confidence in salvation, as with anything else in the spirit realm, is the result of believing with all our heart something God has said. Another Scripture dealing with our confidence before God is found in the third chapter of 1 John.

> **Dear friends, if our hearts do not condemn**
> **us, we have confidence before God and receive**
> **from him anything we ask, because we keep his**
> **commandments and do what pleases Him. And**
> **this is his commandment: to believe in the name**
> **of his Son, Jesus Christ, and to love one another,**
> **as he commanded us.**
> **(1 John 3:21–23)**

God's commandments expressed by Christ reveal His will. Whether a prayer is for our needs or for another person's, we must truthfully examine our motive and ask ourselves how the answered prayer will fulfill Christ's commandment:

- Will it draw the receiver to a saving faith in Christ, or into a closer relationship with Him, if they are already a believer?
- Will it cause them to realize the depth of God's love toward them?
- Will it cause love to increase between all involved?

We know very well the difference between praying selfishly and sacrificially. Our heart knows God can read it. When our heart is true and praying with a love motive, there is no sense of condemnation, and we have confidence toward God. We know He heard our prayer, and we will receive what we asked for.

"We Have in Approaching God"

Our approach before God's throne of grace in prayer is only by grace. That is the only way we can approach a holy, perfect God. Jesus told His disciple Thomas,

> **"I am the way and the truth and the life. No one comes to the Father except through me."**
> **(John 14:6)**

We can approach God because we are covered in the righteousness of Christ. That covering comes to us only by grace through faith in Him, making it possible for us to approach the Father in Christ's name. We can never approach Him in our own name based on any false sense of self-righteousness because we have no righteousness of our own. Any sense of self-righteousness is only filthy rags to God. We only have Christ's righteousness.

So when the Father sees us, He does not see our personal sin and imperfections, He sees His holy Son. He is not counting our sins against us because, **"God made him who had no sin to be sin for us, so that in him we might become the righteousness of God"** (2 Corinthians 5:21). The Father sees us covered in Christ's righteousness and perfection.

"If We Ask Anything according to His Will"

How do we know God's will? By studying His Word, which reveals His will. Reading and meditating on it under the guidance of the Spirit has the power to transform us and renew our minds according to truth. God wants us to know His will.

> **Do not conform to the pattern of this world, but be transformed by the renewing of your mind. Then you will be able to test and approve what God's will is—his good, pleasing and perfect will.**
> **(Romans 12:2)**

God's Word tells us what God desires for us and requires of us. We can examine it on any subject where clarification is needed. The Spirit of truth will guide us and renew our minds according to the truth. He will use it to reveal God's good, pleasing, and perfect will in regard to that subject. If we are asking for something in prayer that in truth is only a veiled attempt to conform to the pattern of this world, the Spirit will use the Word to reveal that to us.

> **For the word of God is alive and active. Sharper than any double-edged sword. It penetrates even to dividing soul and spirit, joints and marrow; it judges the thoughts and attitudes of the heart**
> **(Hebrews 4:12)**

He will let us know it is contrary to God's will for our lives. There will be times in our human weakness that we may not know how to pray according to His will. Romans 8:26–27 reassures us; the Spirit intercedes for us according to God's will in those times.

"He Hears Us"

He does not hear those who come to Him in self-righteousness, in selfishness, or in the deception and darkness. He only hears those whose approach to Him is according to His Word: in the light of truth, in Christ, and in faith. Only approaching Him earnestly in faith pleases Him. We must never forget He reads the human heart and knows the inner thoughts. If our approach to Him is not earnest, He will not hear us, but He rewards those who acknowledge Him for who He is and earnestly seek Him.

"And if We Know"

Know is a very important word! To know means to perceive and understand something as a fact. God has always wanted man to know the truth about Him. The book of Ezekiel has the phrase "know that I am the Lord" sixty-five times. He gave man His Word to reveal Himself. God wants to be known. When God created Adam and Eve, He could have placed them outside the garden, in the world, but He had created the garden especially for them and wanted them close to Him. He wanted to build an intimate relationship with them, allowing them to get to know Him and how good He was.

It is interesting to consider out of all the good things God provided for them, there were some things God did not want for man to experience and know. That is the reason He told them not to eat from the Tree of Knowledge of Good and Evil. He did not want them to attain that kind of knowledge because He knew it would produce death. I wonder why He called it the Tree of Knowledge of Good and Evil and not just the Tree of the Knowledge of Evil?

I don't know the answer to that question. I do know that before they ate fruit from that tree, they walked in innocence and perfection with God. They had a clear conscience and knew only good. After they sinned by eating from it, they gained forbidden knowledge that resulted in a guilty conscience. An overwhelming consciousness of their guilt and shame caused them to hide themselves from God.

It was God, Himself, who planted that tree in the garden and made it grow. He was the one who made it appear pleasant to the sight and good for food. God was also the one who made that one tree forbidden. It probably looked just as appealing as the other trees in the garden. Why He allowed it to be there, within their reach, yet denied access to it, I am not sure. Perhaps, it was to test them. Maybe He wanted them to learn the power of the free will He had given them.

I am not sure it is explained completely anywhere in the Bible. I do know He told them what the consequences were if they chose to disobey. Denying them that tree was an act of His sovereign will. That knowledge belonged to Him alone. He wanted them to trust Him. He didn't want them to seek anything in disobedience or try to satisfy themselves in any way apart from Him. If they wanted knowledge, He wanted them to come to Him for it.

Everything God has done regarding mankind from that time to this directly relates to His will for men to know and learn to trust Him. His purpose for establishing Israel as a nation and a special people belonging to Him was so He could use them to make Himself known to the world. When they failed, He sent His Son into the world to reveal Himself and make it possible for all men to know Him intimately through Jesus. To know Christ is to know the Father. In Him, we can know, with all certainty, that our prayers are heard.

"That He Hears Us, Whatever We Ask"

His hearing us, *whatever we ask*, is not a carte blanche to ask for things that violate His holy will and think He will give them to us. This "whatever" is tied to asking "according to His will." In other words, *whatever we ask according to His will*, is the accurate way to understand this. If a natural loving father would not knowingly give anything harmful to the child he loves, how much more this applies to our loving heavenly Father who is supernaturally omniscient. He will never give us anything that is not according to His will. He will only give us those things that help to fulfill His plan for our lives.

> **Which of you, if your son asks for bread, will give him a stone? Or if he asks for a fish, will give him a snake? If you, then, though you are evil, know how to give good gifts to your children, how much more will your Father in heaven give good gifts to those who ask him!**
> **(Matthew 7:9–11)**

"We Know That We Have What We Asked of Him."

We can have complete confidence and full certainty that we have what we ask of Him. It is important to note it does not say, "we *will* have what we ask"! It says, "we *have* what we asked"! This is a really important concept to grasp, because this is where the confidence and certainty come from.

When we already have something, it removes all doubt and questions. We don't have to worry about it getting lost or stolen in transit. We don't have to worry that it might be diminished to nothing or destroyed before it gets to us. We don't have to be concerned that it may be delivered to the wrong person by accident. When we have it, we have it! This brings to mind another promise of God made available through Christ.

But he was pierced for our transgressions, he was crushed for our iniquities; the punishment that brought us peace was on him, and by his wounds we are healed.
(Isaiah 53:5)

The above verse doesn't say, "*will be*," it says, "*are*" healed! Isaiah, who lived seven hundred years before the birth of Christ, was prophesying as if the act of the passion of Christ was in the past tense, and the beneficial healing that came from His sacrifice was in the timeless present tense.

God, who is Spirit, lives in the timelessness of eternity. With God, it is, and always has been, eternally *now*, because He dwells outside of time. His eternal Spirit lives in us, and we are in Christ. This means our human spirits are also coexisting with Christ in the eternal *now*.

And God raised us up with Christ and seated us with him in the heavenly realms in Christ Jesus.
(Ephesians 2:6)

This doesn't say we *will* be seated with Him. It says we already *are* seated with Him! How is this possible? It is possible because in the realm of the Spirit, it is always *now*. It is eternity! We already have eternal life dwelling in us, and His name is Jesus.

And this is the testimony: God has given us eternal life, and this life is in his Son.
(1 John 5:11)

We know also that the Son of God has come and has given us understanding, so that we may know him who is true. And we are in him who is true

> **by being in his Son Jesus Christ. He is the true**
> **God and eternal life.**
> **(1 John 5:20)**

By being in Christ, we are already a part of God's eternal realm. We are already supernatural beings as God's children because we are in Christ and He is supernatural. Jesus told Nicodemus that a person must be born again. That which is born of the Spirit is spirit. That is why He says, **"we have what we ask"** and **"we are healed,"** in the above Scriptures in Isaiah.

In the spirit realm, the timeless realm of eternity, it is already accomplished! As long as we are living in this natural body, it is tied to time, but our spirits are not tied to time; they are tied to Christ. The question is this: Since our bodies are tied to time, how can we see the manifestation of supernatural "now" promises that conflict with what appears in the natural? We will deal with this in a later chapter.

Prayer

Lord, I thank You for the confidence that I have because I am in Christ. He is eternal life; eternal life is already my present possession. I am blessed in Him and know that everything I need for life and godliness is in Christ. Holy Spirit, please help me to walk by faith and not by sight so that my trust is in God's Word rather than the temporary things that appear.

[Now be specific here in thanking God for something you prayed for in the past and are still trusting Him for but have not yet seen manifested.]
I thank You that _____ is already accomplished in Jesus' name. Amen.

CHAPTER 11

Intercessory Prayer, Choosing Your Battles, and Battle Partners

One of my relatives is a powerful prayer warrior with the gift of discerning of spirits. She called me on the phone one afternoon very excited. She began to share a revelation the Holy Spirit had given her having to do with exercising her gift. For many years, she had been in spiritual warfare over a particular situation. It seemed unfruitful, and no matter how hard she fought, she saw no evidence in them of any long-term deliverance. But she kept praying anyway, even though it was spiritually and even physically exhausting.

The reason she was so excited was because of something the Lord told her. He told her to stop standing in the gap in situations of people who do not belong to Him by using her gift to try and protect them from demonic activity. He revealed to her that the demons that are tormenting people are active in their lives by their own personal invitation or free-will agreement. Even if a Christian casts them out, the demons will only return in greater force. There is a parable that deals with this in the Gospels.

> **When an impure spirit comes out of person, it**
> **goes through arid places seeking rest and does**

> **not find it. Then it says, 'I will return to the house I left.' When it arrives, it finds the house unoccupied, swept clean and put in order. Then it goes and takes with it seven other spirits more wicked than itself, and they go in and live there. And the final condition of that person is worse than the first. That is how it will be with this wicked generation."**
> **(Matthew 12:43–45)**

Until an unbeliever accepts Christ as Lord, and He comes to live in them, no deliverance will be effective in helping them. She said this revelation was life-changing for her. She was becoming frustrated and very worn out in constant spiritual warfare, battling diligently for deliverance for those types of people. Now she understood why deliverance never lasted very long.

We had a nice, long, and really fruitful talk that afternoon. While we were still in the middle of our conversation, I knew it was not coincidental that I had planned to write on the subject of intercessory prayer in this book, but I wasn't sure exactly how to start. Instantly, I knew this discussion would be extremely helpful when it came time to write on the subject of intercession.

In the body of Christ, there is a special group of people that have a gifting like hers. They usually identify themselves as a deliverance ministry. They have taken a few hard and unkind knocks. There has been criticism from some in the body of Christ about a teaching connected to deliverance ministries. This teaching contends that even a born-again believer can be demon possessed.

I, for one, do not believe it is possible, because when a person receives Christ, they are reborn spiritually. They immediately receive the gift of the Holy Spirit to indwell their human spirit, and Jesus promised that the Holy Spirit would be with a believer forever. The Holy Spirit, who is more powerful than any demon, immediately evicts any other indwelling spirit. He seals the believer with a seal that keeps things in and also keeps things out. A demon can't break that seal to reenter the believer. There's no way the Holy Spirit of truth would ever cohabitate with a lying demon!

Demonic spirits are limited to what they can do to a believer. They may be able to seduce, oppress, aggravate, irritate, and offend, but all their attacks can only be external. They can attack the body with symptoms of illness, even attack the mind with thoughts of fear. They can whisper all kinds of lies into a believer's ears, but they can't possess or control a person who belongs to God. He will not allow it, and they cannot compete with God!

Demons operate on and are empowered by lies because their commander in chief, the Devil, is a liar and the father of all lies. They are drawn to lies like maggots to a dead body. That's why it is so important for believers to diligently speak God's truth in love. Since the spirits of darkness know they can't touch our spirit, they focus their efforts on trying to defeat or neutralize the truths we hold by tempting us with unbelief. They gain an advantage when lies are believed, then foolishly acted upon, which disputes what the Word of God says is true.

If they succeed in seducing us, like the Serpent did in the garden, they gain a foothold for external manipulation. Their target is human weakness: the lust of the flesh, the lust of the eyes, and the pride of life. They use these to draw our attention away from truth to focus on external circumstances and appearance of things in the natural realm. When that is accomplished, they can more easily convince the person to act and respond in ways that violate God's will.

To try to cast *out* a demon that is not *in* a believer is not operating in truth. Whenever our battle isn't in agreement with truth, we only intensify any external lying hold the spirits of darkness already have. We must realize all external holds of lies can easily develop into powerful strongholds of darkness. They create all kinds of fear, trouble, and chaos.

But to go so far as to say a struggle in this area means demon possession is possible for a believer is going too far! It gives the impression that demons have much more power than they actually do. It gives place to the Devil by allowing the establishment of a lying stronghold of falsehood in the mind. This is an opening for them to manipulate us and elicit unnecessary and unhelpful fear in the believer that directly conflicts with the truth contained in the Word of God.

> **And you also were included in Christ when you heard the message of truth, the gospel of your salvation. When you believed, you were marked in him with a seal, the promised Holy Spirit, who is a deposit guaranteeing our inheritance until the redemption of those who are God's possession—to the praise of his glory. (Ephesians 1:13–14)**

> **Now it is God who makes both us and you stand firm in Christ. He anointed us, set his seal of ownership on us, and put his Spirit in our hearts as a deposit, guaranteeing what is to come. (2 Corinthians 1:21–22)**

I'd be foolish to deny the existence and influence of demons. They have power, but there are limitations on how they can us it and what they can do. They don't have the power to penetrate God's seal on us and get in. They can operate externally through lying suggestions, but if we exercise our free will to reject their lies and turn our hearts to the light of truth, they must flee.

Now, one of the complications we encounter when dealing with this discussion is that there are a lot of *so-called* Christians masquerading in what I like to call *religion suits*. They mimic Christians, develop an addiction to the religious part of Christianity, and habitually go to church. Some even quote Scripture and give a convincing performance, including the use of Christianese. Their language, actions, and attendance at the church fools a lot of people.

However convincing they appear, in truth, they do not possess Christ and are not possessed by Him. All the externals steps are meaningless if they resist *believing in their hearts* that Christ is the Son of God who died for *their sins* and was raised from the dead for *their justification.* This is God's mandatory step, His requirement for salvation. Going to church every time the doors open and trying to look, act, and sound like a Christian is useless if Christ is not living in the heart.

These are the pretenders to whom He will say, "Depart from Me. I never knew you." You can cast demons out of those people all day long. Whether they know it or not, demonic spirits control them and have an open door to come and go, as they will. Such pretenders are planted by the Devil as weeds among the wheat in churches to stir up all kinds of hellish trouble! They create confusion in the church by appearing to be a demon-possessed Christian. It makes it look like the Word of God that says the Holy Spirit seals believers is not really true.

Judas Iscariot was a pretender. He spent three years following Jesus. He looked and acted like the rest of the disciples. Even though he heard all Christ taught, saw His miracles, and may have even done miracles himself, his heart remained dark. He was so good at acting like a disciple of Christ, he managed to even deceive the inner circle.

I can imagine them unanimously electing him the best person to act as their treasurer. They trusted him and thought he belonged right there among them, but Judas never surrendered his heart and believed in Christ. Instead, Judas yielded his heart to the Devil. The Devil entered him and used him to do his evil work. No one other than Jesus knew this about Judas before it happened. Jesus knew and allowed it because Judas had a role to play in God's plan.

If you are so undiscerning as to choose a demon-possessed pretender as your intercessory prayer partner, you are in for some trouble. You are unequally yoked with someone even worse than an unbeliever. No matter how good an actor that person may be, it is impossible for you to be in agreement with him or her in the realm of the Spirit. You are servants of two opposing masters.

Intercessory prayer ministry is important to the body of Christ. That is why it is so very important to be careful when choosing whom you will yoke yourself up with. Pretenders as prayer partners will be praying against you and actually opposing the very things you assume they are agreeing with you for. This might end up doing a lot of harm. I don't say this to create fear but to encourage discernment. Earnestly pray about whom to choose as a prayer partner. Don't be hasty and take the first person who volunteers. Take care to listen intently to what people say. Jesus said that what is in the heart will eventually come out of the mouth. He also said,

> **Watch out for false prophets. They come to you in sheep's clothing, but inwardly they are ferocious wolves. By their fruit you will recognize them. Do people pick grapes from thornbushes, or figs from thistles? Likewise, every good tree bears good fruit, but a bad tree bears bad fruit. (Matthew 7:15–17)**

The fruit of their lips and the fruit of their actions in unguarded moments can help identify pretenders. Even the best pretenders eventually show their true colors if you pay close enough attention. We are not to judge others, but we can surely be fruit inspectors. You will recognize them by their fruit.

Intercessors are called as watchmen on the wall. The Holy Spirit gives them a special gift of spiritual discernment with the assignment to *watch and pray.* That is why it's a terrible waste of time and energy to be distracted with trying to cast demons out of pretenders. Casting a demon out of a pretender without leading them into the new birth is pointless. More wicked demons than the one cast out will reoccupy them.

Intercessors who get caught up in this devilish diversion tactic often tend to spend too much time talking about the Devil. Doing this gives him more credit than he deserves and misuses their function as intercessors. Let me explain what I mean by this statement.

I read somewhere that in the army infantry there is an elite team known as the scout platoon. This job is not one that many can do, because a good scout has to possess very special skills. They must not only be able to detect the enemy without being noticed, but also must be able to do it while remaining very keenly alert and observant of everything else going on around them. Even under the most stressful and dangerous conditions during combat, they must operate without fear. When they have observed what the enemy is trying to do, they must report that information to their commander, who then can make wise decisions on the best way to defeat the enemy while minimizing casualties of his troops.

Ephesians 6:12 tells Christians that our spiritual enemy is rulers, authorities, powers of this dark world and spiritual forces of evil in the heavenly realms. Then Paul lists each piece of armor. At the end of the list of the full spiritual armor, verses 18–20 tell another part of our armor that is a very important piece: prayer. He told the Ephesians to be alert and always praying for God's people. He also asked them to pray for him so that he would have the right words to speak and would be fearless in proclaiming the mystery of Christ.

It is every Christian's responsibility to put on the full armor of God, every day. All Christians should pray for pastors, evangelists, and teachers because they need boldness from the Holy Spirit to deliver the message. They desperately need His anointing to preach and teach in power. They are on the front line, so our prayers act as a spiritual covering over them as they do it, protecting them from demonic distractions aimed at hindering the truth from being proclaimed.

We must all stay battle ready for spiritual warfare, but just as there are specially trained soldiers for natural warfare, there is a team of unique warriors that make up a spiritual scout platoon. These Christians are called by the Holy Spirit and specially trained as prayer intercessors. Their assignment requires an intense level of spiritual discernment. They watch so that they can detect the Enemy's movements while resisting his temptations by remaining keenly alert in the Spirit. Even under stressful and dangerous conditions during spiritual combat, they must operate boldly, without fear.

They must not underestimate or overestimate the Devil's power, and they give him no glory. They know the One who is in them is greater than he that is in the world. Based on their observation, they can lift up prayers to our Commander requesting extra power, protection, and direction be given to His undershepherds. They have the wisdom and discernment to also ask the Lord for a spiritual covering for the foot soldiers in the Lord's army when they see them growing weary. The gift of prayer intercessors is vital in our battle against the Enemy to minimize unnecessary casualties in the body of Christ.

> **Watch and pray so that you will not fall into temptation. The spirit is willing, but the flesh is weak.**
> **(Matthew 26:41)**

Prayer

Lord, as I intercede for others, give me the wisdom to discern all the Devil's schemes. Also, please help me to watch with spiritual eyes and hear with spiritual ears so that I see others as You see them and understand how to intercede for their needs. Help me join with other intercessory prayer warriors who are filled with Your light so that together our prayers can have a powerful impact for Your kingdom in the name of Jesus. Amen.

CHAPTER 12

Prayer and Fasting
New Testament Style

I love to eat and I enjoy the foods of many different cultures! Of course, I love crispy fried chicken and collard greens, with a nice big slice of Tamerick's hot buttered corn bread! But I also love hot miso soup, fresh sashimi and a side of crispy tempura. I love fish tacos and refried beans! I love shrimp fried rice and war wonton soup! I love a tender leg of lamb nestled on vegetable couscous! I love peanut-buttery, African groundnut stew with chapati bread to sop up the gravy! I love spaghetti loaded with meatballs, sprinkled generously with parmesan cheese and a thick slice of buttery garlic bread! I love sausage and sauerkraut served with crisp potato pancakes! I love a thick cut slice of medium-rare prime rib with a fully dressed baked potato and crisp salad with blue cheese dressing!

Yummy! I love dessert, too!

I love sweet potato pie! I love double chocolate cake with dark chocolate icing! I love carrot cake with cream cheese icing! I love a double scoop of Thrifty's ice cream with butter pecan on the top and black cherry on the bottom! I love thick, gummy brownies loaded with walnuts! I love my husband Jeffery's juicy peach cobbler served hot!

Boy oh boy, do I love to eat! These dishes are comfort food to me, and all my senses get involved in the act. The joy of eating begins with the sound of dishes and pots clanging. Then come the sizzling noises from the kitchen as the wonderful smells sashay out to greet me, building my appetite and anticipation of what that first delectable bite will taste like.

When my food finally arrives, I can see the cook's pride in artistic display on the plate. I have to pause for a moment to appreciate it before I lift a prayer of thanksgiving for such a rich blessing. I might even pull out my iPhone to take a picture before disturbing the beauty of it with my utensils.

Then comes the careful prep I like to do before I dig in to eat. I like slathering a hot, juicy chicken breast with Louisiana hot sauce before I pick it up. I have to use my hands to eat it to make sure I don't miss a single meaty crevice, rather than trying to be polite by using a knife and fork. The medley of hot, sweet, sour, spicy, and salty flavors dance joyously upon my taste buds in perfect harmony.

We're so blessed here. Those who realize God's grace in providing us such a variety of wonderful foods to eat have to stop and thank Him in advance before we enjoy a delicious meal. Sometimes, we eat too much and almost feel compelled to ask His forgiveness for gluttony after we finish. After all, there are many places around the world where people are dying of starvation every minute of the day. The hungry would fight for the privilege to eat the leftover crumbs, fat, and gristle on the bones left on our plate when we finish.

Here in the United States, most take the privilege of having enough food to eat for granted. The massive quantities of food we throw out daily as garbage would likely be sufficient to feed multitudes of hungry people in some third world country. Eating in the United States is not simply something we do to survive, as in other parts of the world. We have taken food and eating so far beyond a means of mere survival!

To us, eating is much, much more than something we simply do to live. We elevate food and eating to a culinary art form. To some it is even a career path. Today's epicureans use food as a means of entertainment, artistic expression, sport, hobby, fun, fellowship, camaraderie, and comfort.

Some love to use food discussions as a conversation starter. I know people whose favorite topic with everyone is food. Almost every conversation, regardless of the time of day, begins with questions about the person's last meal and what their plans are for their next one. Most of our refrigerators, freezers, cupboards, and pantries contain enough extra food storage to keep us alive for several weeks without having to make a trip to the market, if push came to shove.

Food, glorious food!

The proverbial fellowship potluck is a tried-and-true standard in almost every church. We can barely meet together to do anything in the church or fellowship hall without the addition of some kind of light to heavy refreshments. Evidently, food is a great people magnet. It works like a charm to draw even the most peripheral sheep into the sheepfold.

How effective do you think it would be if a church offered a free continental breakfast at all their Sunday morning services? What if they let attendees eat all the donuts, bagels and cream cheese, muffins, fresh fruit, oatmeal, coffee, juice, tea, and hot cocoa they could gobble down in twenty minutes or so before the start of each service, free of charge? I have to admit, I for one think it would be really great—and by golly, I bet I'm not alone. I can imagine people pouring in from all directions and sucking those goodies down like a swarm of starving locusts.

Don't give me that frown; after all, Jesus feed the multitudes on at least two occasions in the New Testament. I don't remember them taking up a collection from the people to cover the expenses. The only baskets passed around were filled with bread to feed them. He was also known to sponsor a meal for His disciples. One of the last things Jesus did before ascending to the Father after His resurrection was to throw a fish breakfast for them by the Sea of Galilee according to John 21.

For many churches, food is about more than feeding the hungry. It has been used as a major fund-raising mechanism heavily depended on every year to cover expenses. Chicken dinners, barbecues, fish fries, bake sales, you name it; they've been used by financially struggling churches as a successful fund-raiser to build something or support some ministry. They are successful because people will always find money for a good home-cooked meal no matter how tight funds are.

I wonder how many missionaries we could actually fund with what is spent on even one church's annual food budget? For that matter, I wonder how many Bibles we could send out to the mission field with the money we spend on specialty coffees and energy drinks in a year? Ouch! That hit too close to home. No matter how tight finances get, most of us will find a way to stretch our budget so we can enjoy our favorite tasty indulgence on occasion. The profits for distributors of coffee and energy drinks soar because of our addiction to them!

Okay, I heard that growl! My agenda wasn't to condemn you for enjoying food or trying to put you on some kind of a guilt trip because you splurge on a cup of coffee. I'm not against enjoying a delicious meal or fellowship potlucks at church! Goodness no! The early church met together frequently to eat together. Besides, I love potlucks and partake of coffee and energy drinks as much as the next Christian. I usually make sure to find just the table at the potluck so I'll be near the front of the line heading toward the food. I love food!

Now that I've beaten around the bush, let's get to the real subject of this chapter: fasting. Because I love food so much, fasting is hard for me. I actually wouldn't feel upset if we ignored the subject of fasting altogether in this book. I don't need to do a survey of one hundred Christians to see how many are like me. A survey indicating how few have gone on a fast in the last ninety days wouldn't surprise me in the least. I don't need deep spiritual discernment to know fasting isn't exactly one of the most popular practices in Christianity.

Well, I know it's not my favorite thing to do anyway. I already admitted how much I enjoy my food!

Fasting is just another one of those Christian disciplines that gets mixed reviews depending on whom you ask. That's why I thought it might be helpful to talk about it, especially since not too many other people are. I guess it's not one of the most popular and requested sermon topics for pastors. I was curious how we, as the New Testament, end-times church, are dealing with this issue; especially considering how central food is to our church life and culture in general. I'm not just talking about the United States, but in other places around the world where food is also plentiful.

To be perfectly honest, I started this chapter this way because I was concerned you might skip a chapter on fasting if I got right into the subject. I decided to catch your attention and pique your curiosity by making your mouth water with my yummy food favorites. Then, I spoiled your appetite by dumping guilt on you about world hunger and needy oversees missionaries. I know neither of these subject is a joke. It was not my intention to make light of them or diminish our personal responsibility as believers to care about their plight. My objective was to have an honest discussion on fasting, and if I offended you in any way, please forgive me.

Now that our senses, appetites, and emotions are all back in check, let's chat about the important topic of fasting and prayer. Fasting is intentionally denying yourself of something enjoyable for a designated period of time. You can fast from food and drink, or you can drink only and refrain from consuming anything solid. You can also fast from certain pleasurable activities at the same time as refraining from eating and/or drinking. An activity fast can also be done, all by itself.

As far as I can figure out, there are no rules for general fasting. It's up to the individual, based on a personal preference, and it can be done for many reasons. Sometimes fasting is a medical requirement before a procedure or before a particular blood test. In those instances, the doctor sets the ground rules for the fast. Some people fast for general health reasons, like cleansing the body of toxins or to lose unwanted pounds.

Fasting for spiritual reasons is the kind I want to look at. We must look at God's Word to find the truth about anything spiritual. What does the Bible say about fasting? It doesn't say very much in the New Testament, but there are many Scriptures about fasting in the Old Testament. The first mention of fasting I found in the Old Testament appears to be the occasion of Moses on Mount Sinai:

> **Moses was there with the Lord forty days and forty nights without eating bread or drinking water. And he wrote on the tablets the words of the covenant—the Ten Commandments.**
> **(Exodus 34:28)**

Here are a few others:

> **This is to be a lasting ordinance for you: On the tenth day of the seventh month you must deny yourselves and not do any work—whether native-born or a foreigner residing among you— because on this day atonement will be made for you, to cleanse you. Then, before the Lord, you will be clean from all your sins. It is a day of Sabbath rest, and you must deny yourselves; it is a lasting ordinance.**
> **(Leviticus 16:29–31)**

> **Then all the Israelites, the whole army, went up to Bethel, and there they sat weeping before the Lord. They fasted that day until evening and presented burnt offerings and fellowship offerings to the Lord.**
> **(Judges 20:26)**

When I heard these things, I sat down and wept.
For some days I mourned and fasted and prayed
before the God of heaven.
(Nehemiah 1:4)

At that time I, Daniel, mourned for three weeks.
I ate no choice food; no meat or wine touched my
lips; and I used no lotions at all until the three
weeks were over.
(Daniel 10:2–3)

David pleaded with God for the child. He fasted
and spent the nights lying in sackcloth on the
ground. The elders of his household stood beside
him to get him up from the ground, but he
refused, and he would not eat any food with
them.
(2 Samuel 12:16–17)

"Even now," declares the Lord, "return to me
with all your heart, with fasting and weeping
and mourning." Rend your heart and not your
garments. Return to the Lord your God, for he
is gracious and compassionate, slow to anger and
abounding in love and he relents from sending
calamity.
(Joel 2:12–13)

The first mention I could find in the New Testament on fasting
is Luke 2:37. Anna was fasting just prior to baby Jesus' presentation
at the temple. The second mention is Matthew 4:1–2. It was when
the Spirit led Jesus into the wilderness for a forty-day fast and He
was tempted by the Devil. Here are a few other mentions of fasting:

"When you fast, do not look somber as the hypocrites do, for they disfigure their faces to show others they are fasting. Truly I tell you, they have received their reward in full. But when you fast, put oil on your head and wash your face, so that it will not be obvious to others that you are fasting, but only to your Father, who see is unseen; and your Father, who sees what is done in secret, will reward you.
(Matthew 6:16–18)

Then John's disciples came and asked him, "How is it that we and the Pharisees fast often, but your disciples do not fast?" Jesus answered, "How can the guests of the bridegroom mourn while he is with them? The time will come when the bridegroom will be taken from them; then they will fast."
(Matthew 9:14–15)

Paul and Barnabas appointed elders for them in each church and, with prayer and fasting, commended them to the Lord, in whom they had put their trust.
(Acts 14:23)

(Please note there were a few other verses that had included the word *fasting* in some translations, but the newer translations that had been taken from older manuscripts did not.)

As I consider this subject in the Old Testament, other than the required fast that God gave in the law in observance of the Day of Atonement, the others appeared to be either voluntary or were a corporate fast requested by a leader to be accompanied with mourning, sackcloth and ashes, weeping, humbling the soul, or chastening the soul.

Some fasts were petitions for God to move in power on their behalf for one reason or another. Some were a show of humility and repentance before God in an effort to divert His hand of punishment against sin. Whatever the specific motive, it appears they were all related to the sin issue and involved both mourning and weeping. Celebrations called for feasts not fasts.

As I consider the New Testament, I have to carefully consider Jesus and why He came. All of the Old Testament motivations were associated with cleansing of sin. That can't apply to Jesus and His reason for fasting. When I looked through the Old Testament motives, the only motive He could have used, which made any kind of sense to me was for "humbling the soul."

The reason I can associate this motive for Him is because of the following Scripture:

> **And being found in appearance as a human being, he humbled himself by becoming obedient to death—even death on a cross!"**
> **(Philippians 2:8)**

Before Jesus began His earthly mission, He was lead into the wilderness to fast for forty days and be tempted by the Devil. The Devil can only tempt human nature, which consists of our body and soul. The soul is the seat of emotions, thoughts, and will. Our born-again spirits are beyond his touch.

Nothing Jesus ever did was without purpose. I believe Jesus' fasting and praying in the wilderness for forty days to be tempted by the Devil had at least three reasons:

1. The isolation was to remove every distraction while communing with His Father in preparation of the beginning of His earthly ministry.

2. To weaken His human nature to its lowest point for the temptation. By doing this, He gained even more glory over the Devil, who miserably failed at tempting Jesus' human nature to sin even at His weakest.
3. To teach us how to use the Word of God to resist the Devil when he attacks us in our times of greatest weakness.

The Devil's attack on Jesus was in the same areas he attacks all humans.

1. Lust of the eyes (showed Him the glory of the kingdoms of the world he would give Him in exchange for worshipping him)
2. Lust of the flesh (turn stones to bread)
3. Pride of life (prove His authority as Son of God)

I have heard many people in support of fasting, talk about the benefits of going on a forty-day fast like Jesus and Moses did. They said after they finished the fast, they had more power and spiritual clarity. I've also read about some who claimed medical benefits gained from cleansing the body of toxins.

I don't disagree with any of it, but I think if anyone is going to go on a fast, it is very important to be clear about his or her motives. God does not simply look at the action of fasting; He looks deeper than the action, to the motive for it. That is why I wanted to compare fasting in the Old Testament with the New Testament. I feel if we want to discuss fasting honestly, we cannot ignore the elephant in the room, which I think is the *sin issue*. That means a discussion on fasting has to acknowledge the difference in how God dealt with sin under the old covenant versus how He deals with it under the new covenant.

Under the old covenant …

• Sin was only temporarily covered by blood shed in animal sacrifices.

- The Holy Spirit only could temporarily rest on individuals because of the sinful nature.
- Only a few special people were considered to have had a personal relationship with God in the Old Testament, and those relationships were always based on His grace, not their own merit or righteousness.
- People used fasting as a means to try to gain favor or as a means of humbling themselves before God in a demonstration of remorse and repentance over sin, seeking God's mercy and forgiveness.

Under the new covenant ...

- Sin is taken away from all believers once for all by the blood of Christ's sacrifice on the cross.
- The Holy Spirit comes to permanently live in those who receive the gift of salvation.
- Jesus reconciles believers to the Father, making it possible for them to have an intimate personal relationship with Him.
- Fasting is no longer a way to gain favor with the Lord, because Jesus already accomplished full favor for us.
- Fasting is no longer a way to gain forgiveness of sin by showing remorse and repentance because Jesus purchased forgiveness for us by paying our sin debt with His blood.

Since under the new covenant, God has provided the means of dealing with sin, what purpose does fasting have? Some say fasting is the means to greater power for living godly, but what does Scripture say?

> **His divine power has given us everything we need for a godly life through our knowledge of him who called us by his own glory and goodness. Through these he has given us his very great**

> **and precious promises, so that through them**
> **you may participate in the divine nature, having**
> **escaped the corruption in the world caused by**
> **evil desires.**
> **(2 Peter 1:3–4)**

However, I don't want to throw the baby out with the bathwater. We clearly see fasting is mentioned in New Testament passages. We read that both Jesus and the apostles fasted, so even though it is not mandated, it evidently has benefits. I believe fasting, when done under the leading of the Holy Spirit, can be beneficial to:

- discipline our bodies,
- help us focus our souls (minds, emotions, and will),
- teach us self-control,
- help us control our appetites, and
- help us humble ourselves before God.

I believe fasting can be very helpful in the above areas, so I see fasting as still applicable under the New Testament. That being said, I also believe fasting can be done for the wrong reasons. When fasting is done with Old Testament motives, it is like trying to sew a piece of new cloth on an old garment, or trying to put new wine in old wineskins—both are ruined and wasted.

Jesus totally changed our relationship with the Father by removing the sin barrier that had separated men from God since Adam fell. His blood sacrifice alone is the only work the Father accepts for forgiveness of sin and favor. If we want to approach Him, we cannot come in the old garment and old wineskins of human works of righteousness or animal sacrifices. We have to come to the Father in Christ, through the new garment and new wine of grace, bearing not even the least bit of our own acts of perceived goodness.

When we use fasting as a means to try and appease the Father, it is wrong! First and foremost, we must understand the Father is not angry with us. Jesus has already appeased the wrath of God on our behalf! It is a total waste to come to Him burdened with sin and a guilty conscience in sackcloth and ashes, mourning and weeping, begging Him not to destroy us, as if Jesus' sacrifice for sin had never been made or was insufficient. If we do that, it is as if we are saying to the Father that Christ's precious blood was shed for nothing! Christ is the one and only way to the Father not only for forgiveness but also for everything else we need!

Being in Christ means being in a constant state of tenderness toward God. When we abide in Him, the Spirit reveals areas of darkness in our souls, and we should immediately repent. True repentance is to agree and turn away from sin and toward Him. We are drawn to repentance because of His goodness toward us in Christ. It is God's goodness and loving acceptance that leads us to repentance, not the fear of His rejection and wrathful destruction, like the people who lived under the old covenant lived in constant fear of.

Under the new covenant, Jesus removed our sins from us and promised He would never leave or forsake those who put their trust in Him. When the Father sees us, He sees His perfect, sinless Son, not our sinful human imperfections. To grow in Christ-likeness should be every believer's desire, and it happens by drawing constantly nearer to Him in the Spirit. We are nearest to Jesus when we are walking in the light of His Word and presence. That is what it means to abide in Him and to let His words abide in us.

When we got born again, God gave us the Holy Spirit to indwell us, but He did not remove our human will. We still possess our frail human nature that loves self-satisfaction. We will be living in this body of flesh that still loves the pleasure of sin until Christ gives us each a new body, just like His. Because of this, as long as we live in this body, we will struggle with bending our will to God's will. It is still an act of choice by exercising our free will to submit to God, rather than yield to the things that bring satisfaction to our sinful flesh and human ego.

Fasting helps us with this battle by training and humbling our human will until our appetites are no longer in control and our will is submitted to the control of the Holy Spirit. When we fast while spending time in God's presence, our spirits become sharper and more sensitive to the truths of God's Word. This human flesh is the cross that we are called to bear as we follow Him. We must be constantly putting our old sin nature to death by starvation.

> **Then Jesus said to His disciples, "Whoever wants to be my disciple must deny themselves and take up their cross and follow me."**
> **(Matthew 16:24)**

> **For we know that our old self was crucified with him so that the body ruled by sin might be done away with, that we should no longer be slaves to sin.**
> **(Romans 6:6)**

> **Those who belong to Christ Jesus have crucified the flesh with its passions and desires.**
> **(Galatians 5:24)**

> **Put to death, therefore, whatever belongs to your earthly nature: sexual immorality, impurity, lust, evil desires and greed, which is idolatry.**
> **(Colossians 3:5)**

New Testament fasting helps in crucifying the old nature by denying our appetites sustenance. It is a proclamation of independence from slavery to the lust of our sinful flesh, to total dependence on God. We are new creations; our lives are hidden with Christ in God. Under the new rule of the Holy Spirit, we no longer live by bread alone, but by every word of truth that comes from the mouth of God.

I am certain based on the teachings of the apostles that the motive for their fasting and praying aligned with these New Testament concepts and was never done under Old Testament standards. Fasting quieted the voice of their soulish human nature so that their spirits could more clearly hear the Holy Spirit's voice in prayer. They needed to know and obey God's will as He used them to build and shepherd His church.

In summary, New Testament fasting is as different from Old Testament fasting as day is from night. In Christ, fasting is a form of worship, and it is very spiritual. It is a very personal decision, an intimate issue between God and the individual. Only God can reveal His will about a fast and give guidance, removing any temptation to use it as some kind of spiritual bargaining chip.

When our motives are not based on New Testament truth, fasting is nothing more than a work of the flesh. Fasting can never bring us forgiveness, access, or favor from God! Forgiveness comes through the blood of Jesus alone. Being in Him provides us all the access we could ever need and all the favor with the Father we could ever want! Jesus is the way, and the truth, and the life. There is no other way to the Father. Christ presented Himself as the final sacrifice for sin, and it is only by grace through faith in Him that the Father accepts us. We are already seated with Christ in heavenly places.

I am an advocate of fasting, but I want to make it perfectly clear that even the most sincere fast is completely void of truth or any spiritual benefit when it tries to do for us what Christ has already done. Those kinds of fasts have the same physical benefit as dieting or exercising. Practicing physical discipline can make us feel very proud of ourselves, and make our bodies feel better, but all the fasting, mourning, and sackcloth and ashes in the world can't possibly bring us any closer to God than what Jesus accomplished when He shed His blood and said, **"It is finished."** Obedience to the truth about who we are in Christ is better than any sacrifice of fasting.

Let's not allow anyone to put guilt or shame on us about fasting, one way or the other. Instead, let's be thankful to Christ for all He has done for us and enjoy our daily bread, as we humbly seek His face every day. When God wants us to fast, He will guide us by His Spirit, the same way He guided Christ.

Prayer

Now it's your turn to personally talk to the Lord about fasting. Ask Him to draw you close to Himself and let you know His will about fasting. He will reveal why to fast, when to fast, how to fast, and how long to fast. Then whatever He tells you to do, just do it. There is no need to make an announcement to everyone. Just keep it to yourselves. Simply and quietly just obey!

CHAPTER 13

The Power of Praying the Word

I enjoy praying and studying the Word more than anything. The more I do them together, the more of God's power and revelation I experience. When I was near the completion of this book, I was invited by a couple of sisters to attend a new early-morning prayer meeting being held at church. Although my preference is spending time in study of the Word and prayer in the solitude of my home, I realize church prayer meetings are beneficial and very, very important to the body of Christ as a whole.

As I already mentioned, I am just not much of a morning person. However, I believe our coming together to pray in agreement as the body of Christ can be very beneficial. So, I set my alarm and decided to go to the gathering one Tuesday morning.

There weren't a lot of people present that early morning, but when I entered I could hear those who were there loudly praising the Lord. They were lifting up their individual supplications to Him as they poured out their hearts. I went to the altar and started to pray, but it was a bit difficult to concentrate with all the mix of voices, including some who were diligently praying in tongues. So, I decided to move farther away from the action at the front to a much quieter, back row of the church, where I bowed down over a chair.

I still couldn't focus with all that was going on, so I asked the Spirit to guide me into God's presence. Suddenly, I heard the voice of the Spirit respond to my request by clearly saying, *Pray the Word. There is power in praying the Word.* I began praying Scriptures by memory. Unfortunately, I hadn't brought my Bible into the sanctuary; I'd accidentally left it in the car, and I was running out of memory verses. When I found myself repeating verses, the Spirit reminded me that the nearby usher's closet usually had several abandoned Bibles on the shelf.

He directed me to a black, leather-bound Bible on the lost-and-found shelf to use in prayer. When I went back to my seat, the Bible fell open to the book of Jeremiah, so I stood up and began reading the Scriptures aloud as I walked around the perimeter of the sanctuary. His presence instantly lifted me up into the heavenly realm. It was glorious! One of the sisters who had invited me was sitting on a front pew, and she sensed the Spirit's stirring and rejoiced in His Word with me as I read. There was no doubt that the Spirit was controlling everything as His spoken Word filled the sanctuary.

When the prayer meeting ended and it was time to leave, I headed back to put the Bible back, but the Spirit stopped me in my tracks and said, *Before you put it back, why not look inside and see whom this Bible belongs to?* I opened the front page and was startled to read the familiar handwritten note: Candice Marlene Thomas was ordained into the ministry by Lillie Belle Lyles on March 16, 2014, at 8:00 a.m.

It was my name, and this note was in my own handwriting. Below it was an almost illegible signature of a very unsteady hand: Ordained by Lillie B. Lyles, March 16, 2014. That was followed by my personal signature and date.

I was overwhelmed when I realized this was actually my Bible. I have several black leather-bound Bibles, and I apparently had accidentally left this one at church a few months earlier. I didn't miss it and forgot all about it. I ran to the altar with the Bible held closely to my breast and fell on my face, weeping and sobbing as I recalled the morning I wrote that note.

I had gone to Georgia to spend the month of March with my mother. She lived with my sister Retta, and her health was quickly failing. The doctors warned that she didn't have much longer to live. I wanted to see her and help care for her needs. Our routine was to alternate caregiving for our mother by taking turns. She would take one day, and I would take the next.

The morning of March 16 was my turn, and after completing her morning hygiene, I began praying with her and reading from the Bible. We both enjoyed this time together. When I finished, she told me she believed I had God's calling on my life. She said she always believed one of her children would be a minister.

Then, almost out of nowhere, she said to me, "You know what, Candy? I just realized something; I can ordain you because I was ordained as a minister along with my second husband in 1967. Do you want me to ordain you?" I quickly responded, "Yes. I would consider it a great honor if you did that for me."

With the sweetness of an angel, my precious elderly mother lifted one wrinkled, unsteady hand toward heaven, and with the other she took hold of my hand. In her weakened voice, she spoke a powerful prayer of ordination over me that morning, followed by a long, loving embrace.

When it was over, I wiped both her tears and mine away, and I realized something very life-changing had just taken place, which should be documented. The Holy Spirit prompted me to immediately make the notation in her Bible, the one I read from. It was one of those life occurrences that you never want to forget. I recorded and dated the occasion in the cover of her Bible, and we both signed it.

When it was time to return home to California at the end of March, I asked her if I could keep her Bible, and she agreed. I put it in my handbag so I could read it on the airplane on my trip back home. When I got home, I went to my home church that following Sunday, took the Bible out of my purse for the sermon, and accidentally left it behind on my seat. Months passed. I didn't miss the Bible or think about that day of my mother's ordination of me.

My loving mother went to be with the Lord on July 13, 2014. As I was grieving her loss, I kept thanking God for blessing me with such a wonderful mother. I relived the wonderful month we had spent together earlier that year and the special time we spent together. Even so, I still didn't realize I was missing that Bible. It was the Holy Spirit in a sovereign act of God's grace who led me to that lost Bible in November of 2014 to reveal an important fact to me.

Although I may have not understood the full significance of what she had done for me that morning, eight months before, God did. He let me know in a most loving and gentle way that my precious mother's ordination of me by faith on March 16, 2014, was recognized and recorded in heaven that very day. My eyes were still filled with tears as I left that morning prayer meeting. I was so moved in my spirit, I decided I would never be without this special Bible. I would carry it everywhere with me as a reminder of my precious mother's reinforcement of God's calling in my life.

As I drove home, the Spirit reminded me that according to His Word, His gifts and calling are without repentance. He reassured me in a powerful, loving way that I didn't need to chase after the approval and affirmation of men for His calling in my life. Depending on the approval of men can be a hindrance to doing His will.

He reminded me that even Christ was rejected. The people in His hometown could only see Him as a lowly carpenter, Joseph and Mary's son. So, I was not to covet acceptance by anyone or allow the rejection or dismissal of others to diminish the value of His call on my life.

It was real, and my Holy Ghost–filled mother was all the confirmation and affirmation I needed to diligently do what He had called me to do. As I type this, I can only say that God is so good. His mercy endures forever. He never forgets His promises, and His truth endures from one generation to the next. He also told me to add this testimony as an additional chapter in this book and title it, "The Power of Praying the Word."

> **In the beginning was the Word, and the Word**
> **was with God, and the Word was God. He was**
> **with God in the beginning. Through him all**
> **things were made; without him nothing was**
> **made that has been made. In him was life, and**
> **that life was the light of all mankind. The light**
> **shines in the darkness, and the darkness has not**
> **overcome it.**
> **(John 1:1–5)**

God's Word is very powerful. He used His Word to create all things. Then He wrapped His Word in human flesh and sent Him into the world to manifest His glorious light in redeeming mankind, who had been disfigured by the darkness of sin.

> **The Word became flesh and made His dwelling**
> **among us. We have seen his glory, the glory of the**
> **one and only Son, who came from the Father, full**
> **of grace and truth.**
> **(John 1:14)**

The light of truth never fails to dispel the darkness of sin. Jesus modeled that concept for us very clearly when He was tempted by the Devil. He didn't whoop and holler in an argument with Satan. He simply spoke the Word of Truth to defeat every one of Satan's lies. God's Word has the power to do the same today! That is powerful! Satan is a liar, and what defeats him is truth. The Word of God is the powerful sword of the Spirit that can pull down any lying stronghold.

For that reason, I consider this chapter one of the most important chapters in this whole book! I don't think we really grasp just how powerful God's Word is! God is eternal, and every word He has spoken is eternal. His Word is as powerful now as it was when God first uttered it!

The grass withers and the flowers fall, but the word of our God endures forever.
(Isaiah 40:8)

In Chapter 8, we learned that praying in the name of Jesus is operating in the authority He gave us to accomplish His will. Although God's will baffles some people, knowing the will of God does not have to be at all confusing. Those who don't grasp the will of God think He gave us prayer to be used as a means of getting our will to be done on earth, but Jesus told His disciples to pray to the Father asking, "Thy will be done on earth as it is in heaven."

We discussed "Thy will be done" thoroughly in Chapter 7, so there's no need to rehash that information. Suffice it to say, God wants us to know His will, so He clearly discloses it in His Word. When we carefully and prayerfully study His Word, we can discover God's will for the world, for the nation of Israel, for the church, and for each of us as individuals.

What I want us to focus on in this chapter is the connection between the power of God's Word and prayer. There is a very powerful correlation that many are missing; one that God wants us to grab hold of as firmly as the early church did when the Spirit originally birthed it.

After they had prayed, the place where they were meeting was shaken. And they were filled with the Holy Spirit and spoke the word of God boldly.
(Acts 4:31)

This order of prayer, the move of the Spirit, and the Word of God are not coincidental. God's order of things is always purposeful. God gave us His Word to guide us to truth:

> **All scripture is God-breathed and is useful for**
> **teaching, rebuking, correcting and training in**
> **righteousness.**
> **(2 Timothy 3:16)**

Because Scripture is "God-breathed," it is impossible for God's Word to ever fail. Everything that flows from God is divine and full of life.

> **So is my word that goes out of my mouth: It**
> **will not return to me empty, but will accomplish**
> **what I desire and achieve the purpose for which**
> **I sent it.**
> **(Isaiah 55:11)**

When I read the following verse, it nearly floored me:

> **I will bow down toward your holy temple and**
> **will praise your name for your unfailing love**
> **and your faithfulness, for you have so exalted**
> **your solemn decree that it surpasses your fame.**
> **(Psalm 138:2).**

God's Word is His solemn decree! God's Word is as good as His name. It is backed by His name and His reputation of faithfulness. Because of God's faithfulness, we can stand on His Word in full assurance of faith.

> **Now faith is confidence in what we hope for and**
> **assurance about what we do not see.**
> **(Hebrews 11:1)**

> **By faith we understand that the universe was
> formed at God's command, so that what is seen
> was not made out of what was visible.**
> **(Hebrews 11:3)**

Today, by faith we need to understand that God is still making the unseen seen. Speaking of His making Abraham a father of many nations in his old age, God's Word says,

> **God who gives life to the dead and calls into
> being things that were not.**
> **(Romans 4:17)**

God has not changed. He is the same yesterday, today, and forever. By praying God's Word out loud, we are agreeing with Him. We are declaring that we walk by faith and not by sight. When we pray God's Word, we are doing the same thing Jesus did when He walked among men. We are not speaking on our own; we are saying what we have heard the Father say in His Holy Word!

In Jeremiah, He said to the prophet Jeremiah, **"I have put my words in your mouth"** (1:9). Then He later says, **"I am watching to see that my word is fulfilled"** (1:12).

God is still putting His Word in the mouths of those He calls. He is calling us to pray His Word in the power of the Holy Spirit because God's Word is the mighty sword of the Spirit. It is sharper than any two-edged sword!

> **The weapons we fight with are not the weapons
> of the world. On the contrary, they have divine
> power to demolish strongholds."**
> **(2 Corinthians 10:4)**

When we declare His truth faithfully in prayer, every principality and power hears it, and His Word tears down and destroys lying strongholds! I'll say it again: there is power in praying the Word of God!

God is not only watching over His Word to see that it is fulfilled, at this very moment, He is also dispatching powerful angels to accomplish His Word.

> **"Praise the Lord, you his angels, you mighty ones who do his bidding, who obey his word."**
> **(Psalm 103:20)**

I also believe that there are recording angels watching and recording our words. In Matthew 12:37 Jesus said that by our words we will either be justified or condemned.

Later in Matthew 16:11–20, Jesus asked His disciples what people were saying about who He was and then asked who *they* said He was. What we say about Jesus is vitally important, not just in the act of acceptance of Him for salvation, but in how we communicate and work out our salvation in our daily lives. The Scripture warns us that we will one day have to give an account for every word we have spoken. That is why it is so important that we be very careful to speak God's truth, rather than our opinions.

If we want to see God's will fulfilled in our lives and in the lives of others, we must both speak and pray God's Word over every situation. What we say shows whether we are walking by faith or by sight.

Prayer

Lord, I know there is power in praying Your Word. You used Your Word to create, and You are still maintaining all You created by the power of Your Word. Help me to speak the power of Your creative truths into the circumstances of my life. [Now consider something you need from God and find Scriptures that address it, praying those Scriptures back to God.] You spoke those words from heaven, Lord, so I say as Jesus instructed us, "Your kingdom come and Your will be done on earth as it is in heaven." I thank You, in Jesus' name. Amen.

PART FOUR

Having Ears to Hear

CHAPTER 14

The Power of Listening

Every successful conversationalist knows listening is powerful. When we recognize prayer as a conversation, it becomes very clear how important listening is to being successful in communicating with God. If we don't really see prayer this way, we'll tend to babble on and on until we run out of things to say. It won't even occur to us there's a need to stop and listen. Stopping and listening is vitally important. We are living in the last days and the Holy Spirit is speaking, but how many of the body of Christ are actually listening or, for that matter, even know how to listen?

The book of Revelation in the first three chapters is Christ's message to seven churches in Asia Minor. The end-time church can learn much from these fundamental truths. Irrespective of the doctrinal point of view on how to interpret the book of Revelation, it is clear God put great importance on listening in His messages to the churches. He gave this insight for our application. The following words are repeated over and over:

> **Whoever has ears, let them hear what the Spirit
> says to the churches.**
> **(Revelation 2:7, 11, 17, 29; 3:6, 13, 22)**

Because of the importance of Christians having an ear to hear, I want to share a few personal observations about listening:

Listening Doesn't Come Naturally

Humans are born innately self-centered and focused on self-preservation. We spend most of our day in our heads; we're constantly evaluating how each tiny bit of stimulus around us is affecting us. When we aren't concentrating on that, we're thinking about and evaluating what we have and how to use it to get what we want but don't have.

It is only natural for a mind that's consumed with self-preservation to spill those self-centered thoughts over into our perception of conversation. It's also only natural to presume that the things most important to us are of equal interest and importance to others. When they aren't, we often assume they probably just need to be properly enlightened and take it upon ourselves to bring them into the light.

Needless to say, if we primarily consider conversation as the means to getting our point of view communicated, this kind of attitude will not be conducive to listening. Naturally talkative people are usually naturally poor listeners. Believe me, I know because I'm naturally talkative!

Listening Transfers Value from Self to the Person Speaking

The most valuing thing we can do for anyone is to listen to him or her. When you value the person you are conversing with, you value his or her opinion. This state of valuing another automatically makes you a good listener when you converse with others. You will also make it a point to remember what they say so you can think about it later.

When you don't value the person you're conversing with, you won't value his or her opinion. He or she may say many words, but most of it sounds a lot like, "blah, blah, blah ... yada, yada, yada." You won't remember much of anything said in the conversation. If anyone asks you for details about that conversation later, you'll probably find it quite difficult to provide anything substantive.

Those who only value themselves and their opinion on things have a real struggle listening to anyone. They are difficult to have a conversation with. You can tell early into it, that they aren't really interested in your point of view or much of anything you're saying. When they aren't talking, or are interrupting you, they aren't listening to you. You can see they're too preoccupied thinking ahead to what they want to say next to bother listening. Their impatience at waiting for the opportunity to say it causes constant interruptions.

Listening Shows a Desire to Learn from Others

Listeners are learners. They've carefully fine-tuned their listening skills because they're eager to gain new information. They like hearing someone say something they don't already know, and their well-developed memories allow them to recall almost everything said to them. Some can repeat, verbatim, something said to them years ago. It can be so long after the fact that the speaker may have forgotten they even said it.

Good listeners also know how to listen between the lines to what isn't said. It doesn't escape them that much of communication isn't verbal. They understand that people communicate as much or more through body language, facial expressions, and with their eyes than with their words. So they listen with discernment, using all their senses. This makes good listeners great prayer intercessors!

Listening Is a Spiritual Discipline Developed over Time

Natural listening doesn't come "naturally" for most. It is learned behavior that takes discipline and practice. Neither does supernatural listening come supernaturally. It also is spiritually learned and takes spiritual discipline and practice. The Holy Spirit teaches us how to listen spiritually so we can develop the discipline of listening to God in prayer. When we do this, it transfers value from self to God and indicates a sincere desire to learn from Him.

But there are degrees of listening. The strength of our spiritual listening skill is based on our development of spiritual focus. Spiritual listening is also called spiritual discernment. It is a proactive process requiring discipline and sensitivity to the Holy Spirit.

What should we do if we're trying to listen in prayer but can't hear anything?

Well, what would you do in a conversation if you were listening but you couldn't hear? You might either a) get closer and remove any barriers in the way, or b) try to pay closer attention to what is being said.

In prayer, we should consider if there are any barriers or blockages diminishing our ability to hear. The Bible tells us prayer must be in the Spirit and in truth. To maximum our hearing we have to keep our spiritual ears open by staying in the Spirit, and make sure we aren't intentionally plugging up our ears because we don't want to hear (obey) truth that convicts and will require change.

What should we do if we're listening in prayer but hear something we don't understand?

Well, what would you do in a conversation if you were listening and heard something you didn't understand? You would a) stop and ask for clarification, or b) write down the remark and meditate on it later until you did understood.

We have learned that prayer is a conversation, and as a conversation it's very clear how important listening is to being successful at it. If we don't really see prayer this way when we run out of things to say to God, we end with an "Amen" and quickly move on to the next thing on our agenda.

Sometimes in prayer, God does all the talking and I just listen and respond. Other times, I do more talking, and He listens then responds. This brings me to a very important element of listening in prayer that I want to share with you. It's something that has revolutionized my relationship with the Lord. I consider it so vital to prayer, I've decided to separate it into a chapter of its very own: "The Power of Prayer Journaling."

Prayer

Listening to God is a very important part of praying, so take some time and quiet yourself. Tell the Holy Spirit that you want to have an ear to hear, and then ask Him to speak to you.

CHAPTER 15

The Power of Prayer Journaling

I've been journaling for a very, very long time. I don't even remember when, how, or why I first started. The earliest writing effort I can recall is a poem that goes back to my days as a young adult. I think journaling for me today originally began by writing poetry. I can't remember all of this poem, but it went something like this:

> I've seen a brilliant light in the midnight gloom of
> my mind's eye.
> A light that's growing stronger day by day.
> Illuminating hidden doubts and fears I didn't know
> I had.
> Replacing their dark shadows is bright new hope
> for my future.
> I never dreamed I could ever be so happy.
> A new day is dawning in the springtime of my life.

I also don't remember exactly what was going on in my life when I wrote this poem, but I think I wrote it over forty years ago in the early seventies

I was born in 1950, and I grew up in a small town as the fourth of six children. We were a proud but economically challenged African American family. My parents got divorced when my mother was six months pregnant with the last of the six children. I can remember the day mom came home from her janitorial job at a local bank downtown. Her arms were filled with bags of groceries, and the announcement was rather nonchalant: "Me and your father are getting divorced."

I was twelve years old at the time of this announcement. My two older sisters and older brother were already off living on their own, so it was up to me to help my mom look out for my six-year-old brother and my soon-to-arrive little sister. I didn't quite know how to respond or process this startling revelation, so I didn't say anything.

My father wasn't very good at being a daddy. I loved him anyway, although I saw very little of him. I guess I was in love with the idea of a father more than the reality of having one. All I can remember about him was that he seemed mostly preoccupied with other interests in his life. Gambling and drinking took up his extra time when he wasn't working as a self-employed carpenter.

I have many warm memories of Mom around the house with us kids, cooking together, sitting at the kitchen table eating, talking, going on picnics at a local park. Every Sunday evening, we'd gather in front of our black-and-white TV in the living room and watch Ed Sullivan. Try as I may, I can't recall my father ever being with us in any of those scenes. It seemed my daddy was always AWOL. I imagine his extracurricular evening activities outside our home fueled my parents' divorce. Even so, I was crazy about my daddy.

I really wanted him in my life, so after their divorce, I spent the rest of my youth chasing after him. I'd frequently drop by his nearby apartment and try to get him to commit to buying me a new pair of shoes or whatever I needed at the time. I really just wanted him to be a part of my life, but much to my disappointment, none of my efforts at reaching out to him succeeded.

It took many years to figure out he couldn't help being distant. Unfortunately, my daddy was emotionally unavailable. I think the biggest enabler for his unavailability was his addiction to alcohol. Just about every time I saw him, he was either drunk, in the process of getting drunk, or passed out trying to get over being drunk. In the final two decades of his life, it was like he was running away from something with all his might.

I never was able to figure out what he was running from, but evidently it was tormenting him. Even with all his faults, nothing could stop me from loving and needing my daddy and the security of his love, but he just didn't have it in himself to give. This left a serious void in my life that I did my best to fill with things and relationships, but nothing worked for very long. Nothing in the world can replace a daddy's love—nothing.

I was a young adult when my daddy died, but to this day I've never stopped feeling the loss a relationship we never had. My personal experience of not knowing my father's love is what convinced me of the importance of fathers. They are like an emotional anchor for their children; an important foundation necessary to build a child's sense of identity and place in the world.

That is one of the many reasons I am so thankful to God for the love of my mother. Although my father couldn't be there for me, she was always there. At the time, I didn't understand why she was so frustrated by my insistence on chasing after my daddy as a young girl. Now I realize that she was trying to protect me from the disappointment and heartbreaks so familiar to her life.

She never complained about it, but I learned later in life that she had a very hard life as a child growing up during the Depression. She also had a very tough life when she was married to our dad. I think those experiences were what transformed her small frame into such a powerhouse of strength and love. Her trials only made her more determined to give us all the love and security she missed receiving as a child, and it mattered little what it cost her in sacrifice to provide what we needed.

I always knew her faith was the source of her strength, and I could see she loved God with her whole heart because she lived out her faith in way that rooted all six of us children. She brought us up in church, and the reality of God was an important part of everyday family life.

My mother was very loving, but she followed old-school child-rearing principles and sincerely believed telling children too many positive things about themselves would only spoil them and make them prideful. To protect us from ruin as we grew up, she avoided overly lavishing us with a lot of indiscriminate, syrupy compliments.

Since puberty is a crucial and confusing time for children in the development of self-worth, I used people as a mirror to help me discover who I was. The way they treated me and reacted to what I said, what I did, and how I appeared reflected my value back to me, forming my self-image. Needless to say, that value reflection wasn't the greatest.

During puberty, children seem to relish in tormenting each other by exaggerating even the tiniest imperfection of others. Criticizing others deflects attention away from their imperfections. It is especially tough to deal with negative peer pressure if a young child doesn't have a strong foundation of self-esteem to start with. Because of this, children need a lot of guidance and positive reinforcement from the adults in their life. It helps them develop a healthy sense of self. This should never be underestimated, because the course of a child's life is set by how well they navigated through puberty.

At the age of nineteen, I decided I wanted to spread my wings, so I left my small town to go and live with older siblings in the big city. It was there I finally found some sense of identity. My poor self-esteem gradually changed into new confidence as I discovered there was something special about me, something of value to offer the world. I realized God had given me the creative gifts of acting, singing, and dancing, which brought positive reinforcement from others.

Those who know the outspoken me today find it hard to believe I started life as a very shy and quiet girl. During puberty, I didn't have a clue who I was, so my low self-esteem resulted in me being easily intimidated. I attribute a large part of my self-esteem problems to the rejection of my daddy. For many years, I thought his avoidance of me was my fault. I was convinced it had something to do with who I was as a person. He didn't love me because I was unlovable. Well into my adult life, whenever a relationship failed, I would think to myself it was also just another indicator of that unfortunate fact. Years of wrong thinking about myself led to many self-destructive choices in my adult life.

As I look back, I know my mom did the best she could. As a matter of fact, she actually did miracles, considering how few good examples she had to draw upon. She had been very poorly single-parented by my grandmother. Because of my father's dysfunctions, my mother's single parenting of us started many years before her divorce from my father. She eventually remarried, but my dad never seemed to be any help to her by way of child support or moral support.

Even the very best mother can never take the place of a father, but I never felt neglected by her. She always made me feel unconditionally loved and well cared for. She gave each of us the very best she had to give and never once complained about the sacrifices she constantly made to do it.

Whenever I look back over my life, I stop and thank Him for working through my mother and keeping me safe through her prayers. It was God's hand of grace on me, guiding me through every less-than-perfect circumstance in life.

The late sixties and early seventies was a turbulent and historic time for people of color. As a young adult, I jumped into the thick of what was going on, but it didn't take me long to discover that the party life wasn't all it was wrapped up to be. By 1976, I had spent the last four years of my life unsuccessfully chasing stardom and love. I quickly learned that those two were a toxic combo, to say it nicely.

One desperately lonely night after an evening of carousing and barhopping, I sat alone, brokenhearted and disappointed in my Hollywood apartment. I couldn't sleep, so I decided to watch TV. I was changing from channel to channel until I stopped to listen to the comforting voice of a big black guy with kind eyes on a Christian TV program. His words were compelling, but when he mentioned the second coming of Christ, I was startled!

"What do you mean Jesus is coming back?" I said to the TV screen. It wasn't as if I was a total reprobate. I had grown up in a traditional black Baptist church. I sang in the choir and regularly went to Sunday school, but I never remembered anyone ever saying anything about Jesus coming back to this world! This TV minister said things surrounding the second coming of Christ that pricked my heart.

When he asked, "Are you ready?" my answer was, "No." When the opportunity was presented to receive Christ, I bowed on my knees in front of the TV with tears in my eyes and repeated the prayer for salvation after him, surrendering my life to Christ. I immediately knew I was different. I'd joined the church and been baptized at a very young age, but I didn't understand what any of it meant. After that prayer, I knew being a Christian wasn't about being religious. It was about having a relationship with Christ.

Not many days after that, I accidentally landed a singing gig with a rhythm and blues band who lived in an upper floor of my apartment building. I'm calling it an accident because it wasn't something I was looking for; it just happened. One evening, I heard a band playing upstairs. It sounded so good. I decided to check what was going on and ask if I could sit in on their rehearsal. They let me and were so impressed with how well I fit in with their sound, they invited me to join them on the audition they were rehearsing for.

We passed the audition and were chosen to perform an upcoming USO tour on a ship that would be stationed in the Caribbean. I was excited at the possibility of finally getting discovered. I got my passport, my family threw me a bon voyage party, and I was packed and prepared to leave. It seemed to be a good time to make a quick weekend visit to my sister and brother-in-law's home at a naval base not far away, while I was waiting for the travel details for the ship boarding in New York to be finalized.

That Saturday night, as the three of us sat laughing and talking at the NCO club, I just happened to look up and notice a handsome young sailor standing across the room. I asked my sister if she knew who the guy was. Allow me to digress before I go on with this story and tell you a little about my sister. She's quite a mover and shaker in social circles. She's also the kind of person who knows how to make things happen. If you aren't serious about something you say, you best not say it at all!

Now continuing on with the story, within minutes of my question, all 6'4", 180 pounds of that handsome sailor was towering in front of me, at our table. I was smitten and speechless when I looked up into his eyes, and he nonchalantly said, "Your sister said you wanted to meet me." I can't remember ever being so embarrassed in my entire life! I was both irritated that she did it and happy that it worked, at the same time. The thing I most remember about that night is how quickly his few suave words stole my heart. I instantly fell head over heels for him.

Years later, I realized my weekend visit with my sister wasn't happenstance or even a bit coincidental. It was clear that God's plan for my life didn't include me running off to New York as a brand-new believer with a bunch of musician potheads to sing seventies R&B on a naval ship in the middle of the Caribbean.

At the time, I didn't have the wisdom to understand what an inappropriate choice I had made when I agreed to join them. God knew, so He stepped in with a more appealing alternative. He knew my dream of stardom would be no match for the stars that would come to my eyes when my new suitor presented his offer. Instead of going off on my adventure in the Caribbean, he suggested I stay and become a sailor's wife. Six months later, I was married to my handsome Prince Charming, and so in love, it all felt very surreal.

The whirlwind, fairy-tale romance lasted only a short time before things got turbulent and stormy. Dreamy marital bliss quickly degraded to a frightening nightmare. The dysfunction and emotional torment escalated each year until it was far beyond anything I was equipped to endure at that early stage of my spiritual maturity.

Twelve years later, after giving birth to three children, I was so close to a nervous breakdown that I climbed into my bedroom closet one night and cried out in prayer, "Lord, if You don't deliver me, I'm going to go crazy." God knew my cry of desperation was real, and in an act of mercy and grace, He allowed me a temporary way of escape so I could bear it. He miraculously provided enough funds to leave with our two daughters and relocate to my elder sister's home in Northern California. She lovingly took us in until I found a job and a place of our own. At the age of forty, I started rebuilding my life as a third-generation single parent.

The five hundred miles that separated my husband and me didn't bring our marriage story to a final end. God only put things on pause as He strengthened me in my faith. I started the process for a divorce, but He refused to allow it because He knew our separation was only temporary. In the year of our twenty-fourth wedding anniversary, after a twelve-year separation, God reconciled us.

When my husband and I separated, our youngest daughter was only three. She was fifteen and her brother was nineteen when their dad came back into our lives. The two older siblings were already off on their own, as adults. A teenager adapting to a father figure coming to live in the home after a twelve years absence wasn't easy. Suddenly, everything changed, and the new family pecking order presented many challenges, to say the least.

I had hoped reconciliation would usher in an immediate restoration of our first love for each other, but our relationship pretty much just picked up right where we left it at the time of our split-up. We were in a different place, at a different time, but we were plagued with many of the same struggles. There was one exception; I knew for sure one thing was very different. I was not the same person that I was before.

Twelve years of intimacy with Jesus, learning dependence on Him, had made me grow wiser. I was much more mature in the faith and more rooted in the truth. I was more spiritually equipped to fight for the survival of our marriage than I was when we broke up.

At the time of this writing, it has been fifteen years since our reconciliation. It hasn't been easy. God is still restoring the years the locusts have eaten. Thanks to His mercy and grace, our marriage has survived every trial and attack by the Enemy. July 2015 marks our thirty-eighth wedding anniversary. Only God can resurrect what was once dead, back to life again. God is truly good!

Like many women my age, I have experienced a lot of trials, pain, and disappointments in life. Because of this, even before I rededicated my life to Christ at the age of twenty-six, I've always wanted to be an encouragement to others. Whether married, widowed, or single, trials in life will come. They will make you or break you depending on how you deal with them.

My mother taught me by example how to respond to pain and disappointment. I watched her handle them by the grace of God, throughout her whole life. Mom was always so strong and resilient to trouble. It was difficult to watch her get old and feeble. She was a widow, so my siblings, as they were able, took turns caring for her in their homes when she was unable to live alone.

We watched in amazement as she aged with grace and marveled at the way she never stopped feeling the need to mother us. "I'm still the mama," she'd say if anyone made the mistake of overstepping boundaries. I think that is why, no matter what, she felt obligated to remember every birthday of her children, grandchildren, and great-grandchildren until the day she went to be with the Lord.

She never neglected sending greeting cards for any and every occasion of celebration with a "little piece of money" stuck in them, even when her children more than qualified as senior citizens in their own right. When her shaky hand and poor sight prevented her from writing the cards herself, she would have my sister, whom she lived with, act as her secretary and make sure they promptly got in the mail so they'd arrive on time.

I'm so thankful for my sister. In her usual mover-and-shaker way, she willingly stepped up and shifted into gear to care for Mom when she reached her late eighties. I'll always believe God equipped her with special personal skills of gentleness combined with strong internal fortitude to perform such a difficult task in such a loving way.

She was specially suited to care for Mom's special needs. When Mom worsened to a state of being bedridden, she keenly watched over our mother. It was as if she saw her needs beforehand. She'd spring into action preemptively to make sure everything was in place. I never once heard her complain about the hard work it took to care for our dear, ailing mother even as she progressed into the final stages of her illness. I will never stop being thankful to God for the sacrifices made by all my siblings. I know each did what they could in caring for our precious mother.

I greatly miss my sweet mommy. Her words of encouragement still ring in my ears. She was and still is the very best role model of my life for what a loving mother should be. It was difficult to release her into the arms of the Lord, but I rejoiced in knowing she had successfully completed her assignment. I could almost hear the Lord welcoming her home to heaven saying.

> **"Well done, good and faithful servant! You have been faithful with a few things; I will put you in charge of many things. Come share your master's happiness!"**
> **(Matthew 25:23)**

With each day, I realize my mother's death was not the end of anything; it was only a shifting of the guard. When she passed over, she handed a mantle to each of us. Now it is our turn to make sure we complete our assignment of standing watch over our children and grandchildren. Her godly example and prayers for us throughout our lives was a guide we can follow.

I personally know she helped me through each of my trials, teaching me not to let them break me, but to allow God to use difficult times to draw me closer to Him. It was the testimony of her life lived out in front of me that led to me dedicating my life to Christ. Now the closer I draw to Him, the closer He draws to me, and it is my turn to pray for my children. I must let them see the same example of faithfulness my mother modeled for me, until they are drawn into their own relationship with Him, just like I was.

As a senior myself now, looking back on my life and all my experiences, what I have learned is this. God has always had a plan for my life. I didn't understand why He made me the way I am. From the time I found my identity in my early twenties, until this very second, I've always felt a strong need to share with others whatever He was teaching me. His Spirit compelled me to openly express both my victories and failures in song and drama. I wanted to let people know He was the strength in my life that kept me going and that He could do the same for them.

My inner thoughts, which were too intimate to share with the world, I would journal and share with my Lord in prayer. Somewhere along the way, without my realizing what was happening, He began directing my journaling onto a fresh new path. It started out as just being a means of expressing my innermost thoughts, but little by little, God transformed journaling into His means of speaking to me by releasing revelations after I prayed and read His Word.

The more intimately I grew in relationship with Him, the more revelation He poured into me and through me in ministry. He taught me that His depth of wisdom had no limits, and His love had no boundaries. Journaling is my record of our growing love relationship, which ebbed and flowed with the experiences of my life over the years. Every time I shared my heart with the Lord, the roots of our relationship grew deeper. The deeper they grew, the more He shared His heart with me to bring new understanding about every area of my life.

Little by little, I learned that His Word was the vital ingredient for continued spiritual development. Truth helped me connect the dots of my life until a picture of who He had created me to be was revealed. He was that mirror of self I had been looking for in others, and what I saw when I looked into Him was the uniqueness of the masterpiece He was creating in me. He was doing it all, and there was nothing I could claim any credit for. I am His handiwork, and what He is creating in me is for His glory, to edify His body, the church.

He loves His church and is instilling His love for it in me. I've always enjoyed going to church to hear the Word preached and taught. I love the beauty of worshipping and fellowshipping together with other believers. Nothing can compare with being used to minister His message of love and reconciliation to others. It is a blessing beyond measure to see the light of His glory turned on in their eyes. But above it all, there is nothing more blessed than the intimacy I experience spending many hours in devotional time, alone with the Lord, my Bible, and my journal.

I wanted to share my story with you to encourage hope. I wanted to remind you that God knows and cares about everything going on in your life. All things great and small have a purpose, even if you can't see it at the time. It wasn't apparent to me either how God would use journaling to reveal His will for my life.

Using my journal, I can look back at trials in my life and remind myself how faithfully He worked all things together for my good in the past. What I read reassures me that His hand is working in my present and will always be at work in my future to do the same. By His amazing grace, He used journaling to revolutionize my spiritual walk.

As I said at the beginning of this chapter, about forty years before I wrote this book, I wrote my first poem. I really didn't have any idea what I was writing about so long ago. I didn't understand what it meant until I wrote this chapter. Now, finally, after all these years, I get it and it makes perfect sense.

> I've seen a brilliant light in the midnight gloom of
> my mind's eye.
> This light is growing stronger day by day.
> It's illuminating doubts and fears I didn't know
> I had.
> And replacing the dark shadows is bright new hope
> for my future.
> I never dreamed I could ever be so happy.
> A new day is dawning in the springtime of my life.

It makes me laugh to think that at sixty-four years old, an age when most are looking forward to retirement, I am experiencing springtime—I truly am! Even when I walked through youthful times of dark shadows, when doubts and fears pierced my soul, I somehow always felt the experiences had a purpose. I can see now they were seeds He allowed to be planted in me, watered by my tears. In God's time, He knew they would produce His will in me.

Now, they are bearing the fruit of hope with such an overflow, I am bursting at the seams. His Spirit compels me to share this hope with others who are desperately in need of a word of encouragement. Over the years, I shared every time I had the chance, but it was still very frustrating. I always felt I had too many words and too few ears to pour them into.

Now, God's grace has given me a bright new hope. I can clearly see God's hand was in it all, guiding me through in preparation for this exciting new season of sharing in my life. It literally feels like springtime to me to share these very words with you right now as I present them to you. Like a beautiful bouquet, they're a loving harvest of spring blossoms grown from the seeds my Lord has been planting in me from my youth.

I am truly more content today than I ever dreamed I could be. I know this sense of contentment is not based on life circumstances. Even as I write this paragraph, I am dealing with some significant life challenges. However, I understand something today that I didn't understand in my early twenties. When I was younger, I experienced something, from time to time, which I perceived as happiness. The trouble was, it never stayed long enough.

What I am experiencing in this season of life is much more gratifying and lasting than temporary happiness; it's joy. The joy of the Lord is not like happiness, which depends on life circumstances. The cares of life can't diminish this joy; it is a fruit of the Spirit, which has no limits. His joy gives me the freedom to love others as He loves me. I can love because I don't have to live in fear of being hurt. I can give His love away with the assurance His love will always be there to heal my heart when it's broken!

His joy comes with the revelation that the quality of my life is not measured by what I have or have not accomplished in my sixty-four years. His joy is not based on the world's standards of success. It is measured by eternity based on what Christ has already done for me and is doing through me. Every day with Him brings a bright new dawning of hope, and my union with Him will never come to an end. This glorious joy emits a brilliant light that is just beginning. It is growing brighter day by day, and nothing can ever take this light from me.

This light is Jesus and I will never, ever have to experience rejection from Him. I will never suffer the grief of losing His love. He has promised,

**"Never will I leave you; never will I forsake you."
(Hebrews 13:5)**

If I claimed that I am brimming over with joy every second of every day, I would be disingenuous. My husband would read that statement, roll his eyes, and sarcastically say, "Yeah, right!" He knows me very well; I have faults like every other Christian. One of the things I appreciate most about my hubby is his sensitivity. He knows how to give me space when I need it.

Some days I don't feel so joyful and talkative. On those days, I can be a little bit of a grouch and not much of a treat to be around, so I tend to hide myself away. Those are the times when my journal is very, very important. God uses it to help restore me to spiritual balance. Past journal entries remind me that God's mercies are truly new every morning. Thank the Lord; He's the same yesterday, today, and forever. I'm so glad He never has a bad day!

When I go to Him in prayer, needing to saturate myself in His healing presence, He never says, "Sorry, Candy. I'm not really in the mood to talk with you right now. I've got a headache, and your constant neediness is quite an unreasonable drain on My resources. You better check back in a couple of days when I'm up to dealing with you."

Wouldn't that be awful! I can't even imagine how terrible it would be if God were moody like I am sometimes. How could we possibly survive if His love ran from hot to cold? It would be unbearable to not know from one moment to the next where I stood with Him. Thank God for His Word. It reassures me that nothing in this world or outside of it can ever separate me from His love.

> **For I am convinced that neither death nor life, neither angels nor demons, neither the present nor the future, nor any powers, neither height nor depth, nor anything else in all creation, will be able to separate us from the love of God that is in Christ Jesus our Lord.**
> **(Romans 8:38–39)**

I really feel sad for people who don't know how good God is. He's not just good every now and then; He's good 24/7. Those who don't know God think He's this unreasonable, perfectionist superpower sitting on His throne in heaven, just waiting for them to make a mistake so He can lower the boom on them. Even some Christians imagine Him sitting there closely scrutinizing every little thing they try to do, and saying with a scowl, "Come on! Give Me a break! Is that the best you can do?"

People who see Him like that are too afraid to even attempt to do big things for the kingdom. Instead, they do the bare minimum and try to keep their distance in fear of His all-seeing eyes. They erroneously think they can fly under the radar and hide from Him. They do this not knowing who they are in Him and who He created them to be in Him. Oh yes, God is perfect in holiness, justice, and righteousness. But He is also perfect in love, mercy, and grace toward those who are in Christ. And yes, He has all-seeing eyes, but His eyes are not for scanning the earth to find fault in us. He's scanning to see all the ways He can bless us and be good to us through Christ.

God is not mean, nor old. Neither is He a demanding grouch who is impossible to please! God is eternally good! He is good all the time; and all the time, God is good and it is never too late to fall in love anew with Him!

Just in case you misunderstand, let me say it loud and clear. Even though God is good all the time, He didn't save us and equip us by His Spirit to just sit around talking about His goodness toward us. His will is that we also be doing good works in His name for His glory. We must take to heart the admonition of the apostle Paul to the church in Philippi.

> **Therefore, my dear friends, as you have always obeyed—not only in my presence, but now much more in my absence—continue to work out your salvation with fear and trembling.**
> **(Philippians 2:12)**

Read it carefully. It doesn't say to *work for* your salvation, but **"*work out* your salvation"**. It is impossible for salvation to be gained by work. It is God's gift by grace, through faith in Christ. God knows full well we have no goodness of our own. He doesn't want us to try and generate goodness in our own strength. That's why He goes on to clarify it for us by saying,

For it is God who works in you to will and to act in order to fulfill his good purpose. (Philippians 2:13)

God is the one who is at work generating goodness in us. When we are not feeling good within ourselves toward others or even toward ourselves, He is ever present to pour out His goodness into us, so that we can be good through Him. All we have to do is ask. It is just that simple! He is more than able to meet all our needs for goodness. There is an abundant, immeasurable supply of goodness available in Christ that never runs dry. There is more goodness in Him than we can ask for or even imagine.

The revelation that we have no actual goodness of our own is very freeing. It is oppressing to think that we have to generate goodness ourselves. We know our personal goodness account is totally bankrupt! Christ alone is our only source of goodness. He lives in us, so we can draw on His supply without worrying that it will ever fail.

To be perfectly transparent with you, when I started typing this section, I was feeling a bit "ungood" myself! But as I typed and the Spirit led me to Scriptures on this subject, He began to renew my mind by revealing to me anew the truth of God's goodness toward me. With each word He prompted me to type, He was ministering out of His goodness account to me, filling me up. He was rooting and grounding me in the love of Christ in all its width, length, height, and depth.

Now, I feel like jumping up and shouting as He is filling me to the measure of all the fullness of God! Hallelujah! I am filled to overflowing with His truth. I am equipped to let His goodness spill out in ministry to others. It is His river of living water that gushes out to water the soul that is thirsty for truth.

Can you see why prayer journaling is so important to me? It doesn't matter how empty I am feeling when I begin. When I combine journaling with prayer and the Word, God never fails to use it in a miraculous way to liberally pour out His magnificent supply of goodness, love, and truth into me. All I have to do is open my spirit to Him. He is always willing and available to fill my spirit to overflowing with His light and goodness. He never, ever, ever fails, and nothing in this world, seen or unseen, can ever separate me from His love! Praise the name of Jesus! He more than satisfies! That is why in dark and trying times, I can say:

> I've seen a brilliant light in the midnight gloom of
> my mind's eye.
> A new day is dawning in the springtime of my life.

Prayer

Lord, I open my heart and mind afresh to Your Spirit. I know You want to fill me with more knowledge of Your goodness because the more I know You, the more I can be transformed into the image of Christ. As I begin to write in my prayer journal, please take control and speak words of truth to me that are so full of revelation that I will have no doubt they came directly from You. I thank You in the name of Jesus. Amen.

PART FIVE

While You Wait

CHAPTER 16

Power Waiting

**Wait for the Lord; be strong and take heart and
wait for the Lord.
(Psalm 27:14)**

As a believer, I know patience is a virtue, but the truth is,
I tend to be a bit impatient. I seriously dislike waiting
for anything! So the words "power waiting" seemed
counterintuitive to me when the Spirit whispered it into my ear.
I love my microwave and cook everything I can in it because I'm
always in a hurry and don't want to take time to wait, if I don't
have to. I want it now! I like things to come quick—the quicker
the better, as far as I'm concerned. I'd rather take an airplane to a
destination and get there in a half hour then spend five long, tedious
hours driving there.

I'm not alone in this. I live around other people just like me who
never want to wait! Have you ever been distracted and sat too long
after a traffic light turned to green, only to get a startling horn blast
from the driver behind you accompanied by a really nasty look? No
one likes to wait.

If you are one of those people who despise waiting, you may be
wondering how in the world waiting can be *powerful*. Waiting on things
is pretty much considered a waste of time to those who want everything

to come in a hurry. Having to sit and wait, and wait, and wait on something is a huge pain. *Grrrr.* It literally drives some of us nuts!

The have-to-have-it-now mind-set conforms to the ways of the world we live in and has led to the development of impatient Christians. The anti-gift of impatience is the antithesis of the spiritual fruit of longsuffering. The Bible instructs to manifest it in Galatians 5:22. Today we understand *longsuffering* to mean "patience," a character trait that doesn't come easily.

Patience has to be planted like a seed in us—developed and grown into maturity through the Holy Spirit's power. It should be no surprise; it takes patience to wait for patience to be matured and manifested in our character. I've heard it said, don't be too quick to ask God for patience unless you're prepared to learn the hard way.

All the fruits of the Spirit are powerful. Developing the ability to be patient is especially powerful when it comes to prayer. One of the most important parts of the whole prayer process is knowing how to wait on God. His timing is seldom, if ever, our timing. When we go to God with a prayer of supplication, it has many stages. I once heard someone put prayer into steps, using the acronym A.C.T.S. I truly don't know who originated this, but I am greatly thankful to whoever it was because it's been extremely helpful to me over the years. Here it is:

A. *Adoration/worship*—the step of showing reverence and praise to God for who He is. This is the first step in any kind of prayer. It is how we get into the Spirit so we can enter His presence. God inhabits praise.

C. *Confession/repentance*—the step of agreeing with God about our condition relative to truth. Communication with God must be in truth.

T. *Thanksgiving*—the step of expressing a heart of appreciation for what God has already given us and for what He has promised us.

S. *Supplication*—the step of presenting our requests to God.

The next step is not in the original, but I've added it:

> 1:4 *Waiting in power*—**"Do not leave Jerusalem,**
> **but wait for the gift my Father promised, which**
> **you have heard me speak about"**
> **(Acts 1:4).**

In Acts 1:4, Jesus tells the disciples to wait in the upper room for the gift of the Holy Spirit. Jesus knew the disciples were confused by their circumstances. The experience of His death, resurrection, and ascension were overwhelming. They were fearful of what the future held for them. Would the violent death poured out on Jesus be repeated with each of them?

Jesus had made many promises to them that the miracles He had done, they would also do. When He ascended, He gave them the Great Commission. He told them to go into the whole world and share what they had seen and heard. But first, He told them to go into Jerusalem and wait to receive the promise, which was the power of the indwelling Holy Spirit. How long they had to wait, I don't know. I know they weren't wasting time while they waited for the manifestation of His promise. They weren't just waiting. Based on the following verse, it is evident they were power waiting.

> **They all joined together constantly in prayer,**
> **along with the women and Mary, the mother of**
> **Jesus, and with his brothers."**
> **(Acts 1:14)**

They waited peacefully together in one accord in one place until the Holy Spirit fell down on them and filled them with power. This same Holy Spirit is the only one who can teach us power waiting. It's not a static act of passing time, doing nothing. It's not a waste of time! Power waiting is a proactive and very productive use of time in the realm of the Spirit. Power waiting is the byproduct of a confident awareness that to pray is not something you do to God, but it is a state of being with God. Prayer is without ceasing and without disconnection.

Just as the disciples proactively continued in one accord, in the peace of God, until the manifestation of what He had promised came to pass, so must we wait peacefully, in the power of God, in one accord, until the manifestation of what He promised us comes to pass.

The characteristics of power waiting are:

- keeping our minds in agreement with truth,
- keeping our hearts in full assurance of faith,
- keeping a confident expectation that the promise will manifest, and
- keeping our confession and actions in agreement with what God promised.

I heard a TV preacher once say, "Your miracle is in your mouth." That statement stayed with me. It rang so true because words have power! I'm not talking about using words in a "name it and claim it" kind of greed mentality. I'm talking about confessing the truth by agreeing with what Jesus said and making sure that whatever we say lines up accordingly. Of course it also takes faith to see miracles. This was Jesus' response when His followers asked Him to increase their faith.

> **He replied, "If you have faith as small as a mustard seed, you can say to this mulberry tree, 'Be uprooted and planted in the sea,' and it will obey you."**
> **(Luke 17:6)**
>
> **"Have faith in God." Jesus answered. Truly I tell you, if you say to this mountain, "Go throw**

**yourself into the sea," and does not doubt in their
heart but believe that what they say will happen,
it will be done for them.
(Mark 11:22–23)**

Can you see how Jesus tied what we say with what we believe?
He said that we would have what we *say*! Evidently what we believe
(faith), and what we say (confession), really matters. Faith and
confession are important keys to everything in the realm of the
spirit. We receive Christ by believing in our hearts and confessing
with our mouths. The materialization (receiving) of answered prayer
is no different. The Word says over and over again, the heart is where
real faith exists. Faith is not just religious facts stored up in our
minds. Faith is truth that has been embraced and allowed to sink
deeply into our hearts. James 2:17 warns us that "**faith by itself, if
it is not accompanied by action, is dead.**

Confession out of a faith-filled heart will always be complemented
by action. We won't be anxiously running around, trying to make
happen what only God can do. We will be actively at rest in God's
peace. We will not be saying one thing and doing another. We will
be walking out faithful actions from a faith-filled heart, in perfect
alignment with God's Word.

If our words and actions contradict what we say we believe, we
need to examine our hearts. Our actions are indicating unbelief.
Thinking and believing are two different functions. Let's examine
the thought process for a moment. It will help clarify what I mean.

We in the information age are constantly being bombarded with
data. Our eyes and ears are under assault with information day in and
day out. We accept information into our minds for the purpose of
evaluation. We compare new information with knowledge we already
possess and have assessed to be true. We ask ourselves, "Does this new
information agree or enhance the truth I already believe, or does it
contradict it?" Depending on the answer to that question, what we do
next with this new information is our choice.

1. We can consider the information as new or complementary truth and continue to think about it; i.e., meditate on its application.
2. We can judge it as untrue; i.e., a lie is what is opposite to/ against the truth; then we can discard it from our thoughts as useless.
3. We can determine it is a lie but not discard it. Instead we hit the Save button and store the information.

Whenever our option is 3, we should ask ourselves, why? What benefit can be gained by continuing to meditate on a lie? There may be two possible reasons why we would do that:

1. Either we are not sure the lie isn't at least partially true and worthy of holding on to in our minds just in case.
2. We are holding on to the untruth because we are not fully convinced; i.e., believing in our hearts the opposing truth we claim is true.

When we fully believe a truth, our hearts are so full of it, so convinced of it, there's no room for opposing lies. One way or the other, Jesus taught that what's in our hearts will eventually come out of our mouths.

> **A good man brings good things out of the good stored up in his heart, and an evil man brings evil things out of the evil stored up in his heart. For the mouth speaks what the heart is full of. (Luke 6:45)**

Jesus constantly instructed His disciples to believe in their hearts and not doubt. Believing begins in the mind; it brings life as it enters the heart. Doubt begins in the mind; it poisons the heart. Poison permitted to enter our hearts, sooner or later will be verbalized.

However, if we refuse to allow our minds to doubt the truth, and fully believe it in our hearts, what we say and do will never contradict the truth we believe.

Anxiety is the mortal enemy of prayer. A tendency toward worrying is a big problem with many people. Some are pros at it! It seems they aren't feeling normal unless they have something to worry about. Anxiety and worry are symptoms of a spiritual disease I call "little god syndrome." People suffering with this are often labeled control freaks because of their irritating need to control everything and everyone around them.

When they think things are under their control, they presume they have the power to fix them. So, to keep things fixed, their minds can't stop trying to come up with ways to keep things under their control. They are compelled to think and act this way. Anxiety caused by little god syndrome is the outcome of believing a lie. The lie is that God is not actually in control, so they need to be.

Trying to control everything is doomed to failure. Man is not omniscient, omnipotent, nor omnipresent. We are not little gods! We are humans, locked in time. We can't see into the future to know if our so-called fixes and solutions will even work. We don't even know what the next second will bring! People who suffer with this ailment can never experience peace. Their need to control has developed into a stronghold of anxiety, and it will not let them rest. There is always something new cropping up that needs to be brought under control.

Certainly I am talking about unbelievers, right? Well, that would make more sense considering they are separated from God and haven't surrendered to Him. Unfortunately, some of the sufferers are Christians who don't even realize they are under the grip of a deceitful stronghold that needs to be demolished. I've heard and hold to a saying, "If you're going to pray, it does no good to worry; and if you're going to worry, it does no good to pray." You read it right. I said, "It does no good to pray."

"Wait a minute," you might say to yourself. "I thought this book is all about the benefit of prayer." Yes, this book promotes prayer, so

I will go into more detail about what I mean. Worry and faith are enemies to each other. God only hears prayers of faith, and worry is evidence of unbelief. Worrying and having faith in prayer, at the same time, is impossible; it is a state of double-mindedness.

> **But when you ask, you must believe and not doubt, because the one who doubts is like a wave of the sea, blown and tossed by the wind. That person should not expect to receive anything from the Lord. Such a person is double-minded and unstable in all they do.**
> **(James 1:6–8)**

> **Do not be anxious about anything, but in every situation, by prayer and petition, with thanksgiving, present your requests to God. And the peace of God, which transcends all understanding, will guard your hearts and minds in Christ Jesus.**
> **(Philippians 4:6–7)**

So what's the point of all this? What must we do after we pray to avoid doubt and anxiety? Power waiting is what we do!

- Power waiting is having our heart so full of faith, we utter no verbal contradictions to block the manifestation of what we're waiting for.
- Power waiting is having our heart so full of truth, there's no room to receive a lie.
- Power waiting guards our heart and our confession to insure they stay in truth no matter how many contradicting facts flood our senses.
- Power waiting is a mighty spiritual weapon of warfare. It is firmly standing our ground in the whole armor of God

and having done all to stand; we stand until God's truth is manifested in the natural. As we hold on to the shield of faith, we use the sword of the Spirit, which is the Word of God, to demolish lying arguments and every false pretense that sets itself up against the knowledge of God's truth.

- Power waiting is resting in perfect peace regardless of circumstances.
- Power waiting is aligning our actions with our expectations.
- Power waiting is proclaiming, decreeing, and declaring God's Word out loud to tear down the strongholds of anxiety and worry.
- Power waiting is visualizing the promise by faith, then saying what you see in the Spirit confidently and continually until what is in the spiritual realm manifests in the natural realm.
- Power waiting is confidently walking by faith and not by sight.
- Power waiting is being filled with hope.

Prayer

Lord, please help me to align my prayers to the truth in Your Word so I can always pray in confidence. Then, help me learn how to wait in power for Your perfect timing. As I wait for the unseen to manifest, help me bear the fruit of patience and self-control so that I will bring You glory. I yield my tongue to You so that by the power of Your Spirit, I will speak only the truth when what I see doesn't agree with what I'm waiting for. I thank You in advance for the victory because I know it is mine through Jesus. Amen

CHAPTER 17

A Study on Miracles

**You are the God who performs miracles; you
display your power among the peoples.
(Psalm 77:14)**

I'd confidently say that every member of the body of Christ
believes the miracles of the Bible are true and are not fables. If
a biblically literate believer was asked if he or she accepted the
miracles of creation, the burning bush, and parting of the Red Sea
in the days of Moses, or any other miracle in the Old Testament as
events that actual happened, I think they would say, "Absolutely!"
I think they would also willing go to bat for the miracle of Jesus
raising Lazarus from the dead, along with every other miracle Jesus
and the apostles performed that is recorded in the New Testament.

However, if you asked a diverse group of Christians if they
believe miracles are for this age, *today*, well you would get at least
three different responses: absolutely yes, absolutely no, and maybe,
I'm not sure.

If you asked them the reason for their answer and specific Bible
verses to support their opinion, only a few would be able to supply
them. Even though true Christians say they believe in the Bible as
God's infallible Word, many of our points of view on spiritual things

are as much based on our own personal spiritual experiences and opinion as they are on actual biblical truth.

If you asked the "absolutely no" or even the "maybe, I'm not sure" groups if they believed their salvation or anyone's salvation was a miracle, they would most likely say yes. Some, realizing you may be trying to entrap them, would follow up with something like, "I believe God is still doing miracles like *that*; I just don't believe He's doing the kinds of miracles like the ones recorded during the Old and New Testament any longer.

Those miracles happened before the Bible was completed, and now that we have the Bible, we don't need those kinds of miracles any longer. You could give them convincing arguments and testimonies of miracles you've heard, or even show them documentation on miracles you've researched. You could even share miracles you've personally experienced, but chances are, it would do little to change their point of view. They, like most of us, form the majority of our opinions on personal experience.

The Bible tells us in Jeremiah 17:9 how deceitful the human heart is. Jesus, knowing the human heart, said the following to a man who approached Him, asking for a miracle:

"Unless you people see signs and wonders," Jesus told them, "you will never believe." (John 4:48)

When it comes to miracles, some are a lot like this man or like Thomas was in the days right after Jesus' resurrection. Thomas had heard all the eyewitness testimonies. He observed the joy and excitement of those who had actually seen Jesus alive, but the very idea of a miracle so magnificent was too much for his natural mind to grasp. Thomas' response to everything they shared with him was:

> **"Unless I see the nail marks in his hand and
> put my finger where the nails were, and put my
> hands into his side, I will not believe."**
> **(John 20:25)**

Because of this one unfortunate comment, even to this day, we unfairly label him, "Doubting Thomas." We also label those who struggle with belief in miracles like Thomas did, the same way. However, we must not be too judgmental toward miracle naysayers. After all, Jesus knew exactly what Thomas had said but He didn't condemn him, reject him, and tell him to hit the road. He drew near to Thomas and let him do the things he required to believe. After that, Jesus lovingly said to him,

> **"Put your finger here; see my hands. Reach out
> your hand and put it into my side. Stop doubting
> and believe."**
> **(John 20:27)**

It was Jesus' goodness that brought Thomas to repentance.

> **Thomas said to Him, "My Lord and my God!"**
> **Then Jesus told him, "Because you have seen me,
> you have believed; blessed are those who have
> not seen and yet have believed."**
> **(John 20:28–29)**

Jesus' revelation on the blessedness of believing without seeing should be helpful to those struggling with belief in miracles today. There's an old adage that says, "Seeing is believing." Like Thomas, some say they will believe once they see evidence. Seeing is no guarantee of believing. Faith does not require seeing.

Jesus performed countless undeniable miracles in the sight of the religious leaders. He fulfilled every one of the Old Testament prophecies they knew and studied. Yet those bound up in a religious mind-set who saw Jesus do miracles with their very own eyes, remained in unbelief, blinded to His deity. With eyes that could not see, they refused to repent of their unbelief and accept Him as their promised Messiah.

I believe miracles are for today, but in no way am I trying to imply that this belief is mandatory to prove your salvation. Salvation requires believing in the miracles of Jesus' virgin birth, death on the cross for sin, and His resurrection from the dead, accompanied by the confession of faith. A mental assent to the *possibility* of the salvation miracle through Christ's shed blood has no power to save. A mental assent to truth is not belief.

Truly believing in Christ's sacrifice is to embrace the truth in the heart by faith as God's gracious gift in payment for *our personal* sins. That is the only way we can receive salvation and be spiritually born again. The miracle of salvation is the greatest of all miracles, and it is not the result of natural seeing. It is a result of seeing spiritually by faith.

As believers in Christ, we are instructed that just as we are saved by faith, we need to continue to walk by faith and not by sight. What we see is only temporary anyway; it is the unseen that is eternal. It takes faith to be certain of what is unseen based on the truth of God's eternal Word regardless of what our eyes see. I don't think God's objective for miracles has ever changed.

The purpose of miracles is so that we "not be unbelieving but believing." This would be my response to both the Doubting Thomases of the world and those inside the body of Christ who struggle with believing in miracles. I honestly believe God is still doing miracles today. He wants to display His power among the nations in this day. He needs believers to work through to accomplish these miracles. He has always used His chosen ones to display His power.

Just as He did miracles in the days of Noah, in the days of the apostles of the early church, He wants to do in the age of grace. He wants to display His mighty power through the end-time church in miracles, signs, and wonders because He's not willing for any to perish. He wants as many men as possible to repent from their sins, turn to Him, believe in Christ as Savior, and be reconciled into His family.

It is God who does miracles through men. Apart from His power, all men are weak and helpless. Jesus walked among men as God in the flesh, but He said it was His Father who was doing the miracles through Him. He was simply doing what He saw the Father do and speaking what He heard the Father speak.

He told His disciples that the works He did, they would do also, and even greater works because He was returning to His Father. Miracles and greater works are possible by believers today because Jesus sent the Holy Spirit to indwell us. The same power that raised Christ from the dead lives in us. It is the Spirit who empowers us to live for Him and to do those greater works Jesus spoke of.

> **Now to each one the manifestation of the Spirit is given for the common good. To one there is given through the Spirit a message of wisdom, to another a message of knowledge by means of the same Spirit, to another faith by the same Spirit, to another gifts of healing by that one Spirit, to another miraculous powers, to another prophecy, to another distinguishing between spirits, to another speaking in different kinds of tongues, and to still another the interpretation of tongues. All these are the work of one and the same Spirit, and he distributes them to each one, just as he determines.**
> **(1 Corinthians 12:7–11)**

We should expect Him to work miracles through us according to these promises. All of the things listed in the above verse are miraculous works of the Spirit. They are impossible to be generated apart from Him. Miracles are kingdom work. When Jesus was on earth, He spent most of His time teaching about the kingdom and authenticating His authority on earth by doing miracles of all kinds. He told the people those miracles were evidence the kingdom was near to them.

When Jesus sent seventy of His disciples out two by two, He told them:

> **"When you enter a town and are welcomed, eat what is offered to you. Heal the sick who are there and tell them, "The kingdom of God has come near to you."**
> **(Luke 10:8–9)**

When He ascended to the Father, He told His followers,

> **"Peace be with you! As the Father sent me, I am sending you."**
> **(John 20:21)**

He sent them out to preach the gospel of His kingdom and to do the greater works because He was returning to His Father. We are no less a part of His church than the ones who saw Him ascend into heaven. Just as we believe in His ascension without having seen it, we can believe and expect Him to accomplish His will through us the way He did through the early church. The agenda is the same: to seek and save the lost.

Jesus is the same yesterday, today, and forever. He is still reaching out in love to men, reconciling them to the Father through His blood. He will use whomever He desires and any circumstance He desires to draw men to Him. To be used by God to do miracles, we must not allow doubt or fear to keep us from praying God-sized, radical prayers in Jesus' name, for His glory!

Let's dare to expect Him to do the miraculous through us and know without a doubt His power makes the impossible, possible. There is no limit to what He will do when we walk in faith and absolute dependence on Him.

If the thought of God doing miracles through us makes us feel weak and incapable … great! That is just where He wants us, so we will draw on His mighty power and not ours. If we think we can do the work of the kingdom in our own strength, we will surely fail!

Pride causes men to resist submitting to God for power and grace, but the end result of self-sufficiency will always be defeat, burnout, and failure. Those who depend on self put a large target on their heads, inviting the Enemy's fiery darts. Be assured, satanic powers catch the scent of carnality from miles away.

The Devil has an insatiable appetite for prideful flesh and loves nothing more than to devour it. He knows dependence on our humanity is what makes us weak. Our strength must never be based on what we think we can do on our own. God used Paul to set an example on what to do with feelings of human weakness.

> **But he said to me, "My grace is sufficient for you, for my power is made perfect in weakness." Therefore I will boast all the more gladly about my weaknesses, so that Christ's power may rest on me. That is why, for Christ's sake, I delight in weaknesses, in insults, in hardships, in persecutions, in difficulties. For when I am weak, then I am strong.**
> **(2 Corinthians 12:9–10)**

When we present our weaknesses to the Lord, we find our source of strength in His mighty power, and He will manifest Himself in miracles, signs, and wonders!

Prayer

Lord, I believe in miracles! I know that You never change and are the same today as You were in biblical days. Get glory from my circumstances any way You choose. If a miraculous sign will accomplish Your will, help me by Your Spirit to cooperate with You to believe for it. [Now consider your needs and boldly ask God for a miracle in your personal circumstances] I give You all glory, honor, and praise in all areas of my life in the name of Your Son, Jesus. Amen.

CHAPTER 18

Prayer and the Sovereignty of God

In the beginning God created the heavens and the earth.
(Genesis 1:1)

he God who is, who was, and who forever will be, has eternal supremacy. He is sovereign over the natural and the supernatural! The apostle Paul was a Pharisee before his conversion and a student of the Old Testament. He knew Isaiah had prophesied in Isaiah 53:5 that by the Messiah's wounds, healing would come. I believe he had this Scripture in mind on the island of Malta when the viper bit him, and he shook it off his hand without suffering any ill. I believe he remembered it when he laid hands on the father of Publius, who was sick with fever and dysentery, and healed him. He knew all about God's power to heal.

God did extraordinary miracles through Paul, so that even handkerchiefs and aprons that had touched him were taken to the sick, and their illnesses were cured and the evil spirits left them.
(Acts 19:11–12)

Yet this same Paul who was used by God to heal many pleaded with Him three times to heal him and take away his own thorn in the flesh, but God refused. He told Paul His power was being made perfect in his weaknesses. God, who is omnipotent, omniscient, and omnipresent, ruling in a perfect balance of justice and mercy, reminded Paul that He is sovereign.

Most of us don't think very much about such theological concepts as the sovereignty of God in our day-to-day Christian walk. It's one of those topics average believers aren't likely to be discussing over a potluck dinner. No one likes talking about the reality of pain and suffering in the lives of Christians! Just like no one enjoys being beaten and left for dead, or going hungry.

Even so, at this very moment some believer who loves the Lord with all his or her heart, somewhere in the world is experiencing one or all these discomforts because of his or her faith in Christ. This is not happening because God doesn't know or doesn't care. God both knows and cares very much! This is the seeming contradiction unbelievers love to throw in our faces!

What do you answer them when they corner you with this: "If God is so powerful and loving, why doesn't He do something about human suffering? And if He's so good, why do innocent babies die?" What's your response to that age-old question, "Why does God allow evil to exist?"

People who ask these questions only use them as a defense mechanism to try to shut us up and get us out of their faces. They don't actually expect any Christian to give them a logical answer. In most cases, no matter how convincing or theologically sound explanation of God's sovereignty is given, it wouldn't change their minds in the least; to them it would sound illogical. Faith in God makes no sense to the carnal mind. Only the Holy Spirit can take the blinders from their eyes to cure their spiritual blindness. All the clever intellectual reasoning in the world can't do that.

Just like Paul, sooner or later we all experience our own personal thorns in the flesh and are forced to come face-to-face with the concept of God's sovereignty. The idea of God saying no to us at the same time He's saying yes to someone else can be tough. It gets even harder if both are for the same request. It is even more troublesome if the one being used by Him to minister a miracle is still waiting for the same miracle themselves.

That's when the sovereignty of God isn't just another dry, theological discussion. It's real life and the human mind grapples with reasoning out the concept of the sovereignty of God on a personal level. Trying to understand an infinite God with a finite mind is impossible! It demands faith from our spirit being. The sovereignty of God is unreasonable to the carnal mind.

> **"For my thoughts are not your thoughts, neither are your ways my ways," declares the Lord. "As the heavens are higher than the earth, so are my ways higher than your ways and my thoughts than your thoughts."**
> **(Isaiah 55:8–9)**

The God who created time and has forever existed outside of time has created a timeline for everything regarding man. We all know life can get tormenting, sometimes. In those difficult seasons, I have to remind myself that in His time, He will make all things beautiful. That timing is under His control. The old saints liked to say, "He may not come when you want Him, but He's always on time." The Bible warns us things will get worse and worse, the closer we get to the day of the Lord.

As we approach that day, it will be wise to remember the following: With God, the very second He began time's relentless progression is no different from this very second we breath in air, or the moment in the future when He finally merges all things (including time) into eternity. God is sovereign over time; both the present and the future are now to Him.

A Fantasy Room

Time on earth boxes us in like the walls of a fantasy room. Drapes hang at two picture windows, and we have the freedom to open them and look out. If our fears keep them drawn as protection from the peering eyes of others, the room becomes a dark prison. No light can get in and no light can get out. There are two automatic doors on opposite ends of the room marked, "Enter Only" and "Exit Only." God holds the power control button over those doors. He sets the timing of both our entrance through birth and our exit through death. In the interim, His grace allows us free will to determine what type of occupants we will be.

He supplies the room with hidden pieces of treasure and trash. He expects us to find them and discover ways to use them to create the quality of life that best defines the values we have embraced. Some occupants, selfishly interested in only treasures, find them, quickly grow bored, and then toss them aside as trash. The wise and adventurous diligently search for both treasure and trash. They delight in discovering ways to use treasures as tools to transform trash into additional treasures.

God, in His sovereignty, has hidden the power of time for each to discover and value, as they will. Some value it as treasure and invest it, leaving all things bettered by their presence. Some devalue it as trash and waste it away, leaving only garbage and chaos behind.

*****

Okay. So what does any of this have to do with prayer and the sovereignty of God? Well, in my fantasy room, the sovereignty of God, the Word of God, and prayer are treasures hidden in plain sight. Those who love truth easily find them and understand how to balance them together in wisdom. In the intimacy of prayer and the study of the Bible, God teaches us how to see life as He sees it. When we see through His eyes, we see beyond superficial externals.

What the unenlightened eye discards as trash, eyes of faith see as treasure in the making.

The more time we spend with Him in the intimacy, the more we learn to trust His sovereignty. In prayer, He discloses the wisdom of His plan to every heart yielded to Him. A yielded heart is a precious treasure to God used to redeem both time and circumstance in ways to bring Him glory.

It is impossible to talk about the sovereignty of God without talking about repentance. A repentant heart is a humbled heart, and it is only through humility that anyone can embrace the concept of God's sovereignty. A proud, rebellious heart resents the idea of God being sovereign because a proud human heart wants to reign supreme. It adamantly resists submission to God's truth and His rule.

The fourth chapter of the book of Daniel tells the story of an overly proud king by the name of Nebuchadnezzar. God humbled this king by driving him to his knees. He went insane, eating grass like an ox. When he finally repented, he came to his senses and said:

> **At the end of that time, I, Nebuchadnezzar, raised my eyes toward heaven, and my sanity was restored. Then I praised the Most High; I honored and glorified him who lives forever. His dominion is an eternal dominion; his kingdom endures from generation to generation. All the peoples of the earth are regarded as nothing. He does as he pleases with the powers of heaven and the peoples of the earth. No one can hold back his hand or say to him; "What have you done?" (Daniel 4:34–35)**

> **Now I, Nebuchadnezzar, praise and exalt and glorify the King of heaven, because everything**

he does is right and all his ways are just. And those who walk in pride he is able to humble. (Daniel 4:37)

The end of **Daniel 9:18** made a statement under the old covenant that I believe still holds true under the new covenant:

We do not make requests of you because of our righteousness but because of your great mercy. (Daniel 9:18)

Sometimes, it baffles my mind why God in His omniscience created man with free will. When He created Adam, the Bible says He created him in His image. Giving Adam the gift of free will was giving him a tiny taste of sovereignty, himself. Adam's free will allowed him to decide whether to believe God or the serpent. God had determined in His wisdom to never violate man's free will choice, but He demands accountability and consequences for choices made.

Beginning with the fall of Adam, man has never been able to be righteous in himself because free will is weakened by sin-loving flesh. God in His mercy knew in advance that man would fall into sin, and it is the only thing that kept Him from completely wiping the sin-tainted man and woman He created in perfection from the face of the earth. We all sin and fall short of the glory of God. No one is perfect but Christ alone. When we sin we are exercising our free will wrongly. But because of God's great mercy, He sent His only begotten Son to solve the sin problem.

Christ, in obedience to the Father, took our sin on Himself and became sin for us. He did that so we could become the righteousness of God in Him, but this transfer requires man's exercise of free will. When a sinful human repents and chooses Christ, he comes under the law of faith and receives the benefits of the new covenant of righteousness in Christ. Jesus is sitting at the right hand of the Father making intercession for all those who are in Him. He is standing in the gap, justifying us and giving us right standing before God.

We must cling to the truth of righteousness in Christ with all of our hearts today, more than ever before. We live in very evil days because the Devil knows his time is short. He is prowling about as a roaring, raging lion seeking whom he can devour. He is tempting men's free will to sin against God just like he did in the garden with Adam and Eve. He knows it will result in violence, confusion, and destruction every time men yield to his seduction.

The Devil may be doing a lot of damage, but he is only a created being himself. His power is limited. He is neither sovereign nor in control. Creator God is in control. He is waiting for us to use our free will wisely by calling out to Him in spirit and in truth. When we do, He will deliver our churches, our homes, and our individual lives from the prevailing darkness of this age. The Most High God is sovereign and omnipotent, and as His people, called by His name, we must humble ourselves and pray and seek His face.

We must repent and turn from our complacency and agreement with the wickedness of this present age. God holds our lives and future in His hands, and He wants us to diligently seek Him. He said it is only when we seek Him with all of our hearts that we will find Him. When we do, He delights in hearing and answering our prayers. His presence will bring the change we need, change that begins within us. When we are changed, we will be a light in the darkness, making a positive difference in our communities and in our country through His power that is alive in us.

The King reigns in sovereignty in the hearts of all who belong to Him. As citizens of the kingdom, we keenly listen for the King's voice so we can obey His commands and seek His kingdom. That is why it is so important that we abide in Him and know how vitally important the power of prayer is in accomplishing His end-time's agenda.

It is true that no man knows the day or the hour, but God wants us to discern the signs of the times. It is not His will for that day to catch us unaware and unprepared. We can best prepare for it by redeeming the time and acknowledging there is not much time left to fulfill His purpose and plan for our lives. Each of us has been given an important and vital assignment based on our individual uniqueness, custom made to fit our gifts. He also has given us all the power we need to do them. We will have to stand before Him one day and give an account to Him for how we completed those assignments, and we will have no excuse. If we obey Him now, there will be no reason for fear on that day. It will be a time of rejoicing.

For the Lord himself will come down from heaven, with a loud command, with the voice of the archangel and with the trumpet call of God, and the dead in Christ will rise first. After that, we who are still alive and are left will be caught up together with them in the clouds to meet the Lord in the air. And so we will be with the Lord forever. Therefore encourage one another with these words.
(1 Thessalonians 4:16–18)

The seventh angel sounded his trumpet, and there were loud voices in heaven, which said, "The kingdom of the world has become the kingdom of our Lord and of his Messiah, and he will reign for ever and ever."
(Revelation 11:15)

Prayer

Lord, You are sovereign! You created time, and it is under Your perfect control. Christ, we know one day You will return in glory. The Father will say to You that the time has come to complete all things. When You return, there will be no one able to resist Your power and sovereignty for it is the Father's will for You to put down all earthly rule and authority. Every knee in heaven and on earth will bow, and every tongue will confess that You are Lord.

On that day, the human free will of every man will yield to Your sovereign will. As we wait for Your appearance, Lord, give us the strength to stand and having done all to stand. Help each of us to hear the voice of the Spirit as He reveals our calling and please help us to know that fulfilling that calling can only be accomplished by the Spirit's power.

Help us to realize the time is short so we must be about Your business. We give You all the glory and praise for what You are doing and all that will be accomplished in the name of our Sovereign Lord, Jesus. Amen.

Conclusion

W ith my last words, I will again repeat without intimidation, I wrote this book because I was commanded to do it by the Spirit of the living God. He alone knows how desperately I personally needed to be schooled and reschooled on prayer. I doubt this is different from most believers.

We must grab hold of the truth and understand that prayer is a powerful weapon in spiritual warfare. It is vitally important that we learn as much as we can about prayer warfare in the bright spiritual light of the church. A time is soon coming when darkness will increase and the spiritual battle will heighten and intensify like never before. In the heat of battle, with the Devil doing everything he can to disrupt communications, we must be already tuned in to God and fully prepared for battle.

In an atmosphere of warfare, we must powerfully and confidently use prayer and the Word of God to bring down strongholds of darkness. It will be too late then for "schools of prayer." It will be time for decisive action in the power of the Spirit, not time for trying to learn how to get prayers through to God. It will be an ambient environment of spiritual darkness, but the discerning will have been forewarned. Remember, the Devil is the prince of the power of the air. He rules over the kingdom of darkness! I don't say this to invoke fear but to emphasize the importance of readying ourselves now, while we have the light.

That is why the time for a revolution in prayer is now! A prayer revolution is what I hoped to incite with this book. Did I succeed? Judge me, as you will, but I will not judge myself in this. I will say, if nothing else, writing this book was a success because my personal prayer life was revolutionized. The things the Holy Spirit taught me about prayer drastically improved my whole relationship with God! *He taught me that prayer is all about relationship and communication!*

You have to decide for yourself if you have learned anything yourself and if it changed you in any way. How far it went on your personal revolution gage depends on how the things you've read affected the perception of your intimacy with God. The ultimate test is not what you read in this book. It is what you heard God intimately whisper to you.

I take no credit or fault for anything within these pages. Writing it was neither my idea nor was it my information. I wrote what I heard and was told to write. The title, *School of Prayer—Time for a Revolution!*, came from the Holy Spirit. I believe He chose that title because He was teaching me something new and revolutionary in every single chapter.

He gave me specific Scriptures and spiritual concepts to use. He even awakened me from sleep with words in my mind that He wanted me to put in it—words I'd never used in conversation before. I had to look them up in the dictionary to see what they meant. Then He let me know how to use them in the context of what He wanted me to say. I also count it a success that I was able to finish this book and get it published.

An enthusiastic start and a terrible finish of things have marked my whole life's story up till now. Lengthy writing projects lacked motivation to complete them. Fear of failure always seemed to stop me short. I would hear the words in my ear, "Nobody cares about what you have to say. Don't make a fool of yourself."

Even when I got close to the end of this book, I started to get a bit nervous. I reminded myself that all I had to do was obey God. The only way I could fail would be to fail to complete the assignment

He gave me. The Spirit let me know very clearly right from the start, this was a project that *had to be promptly completed*. He would guide me all the way through to publishing and distribution of it.

When I had finished writing and moved on to my review, I told the Lord that since this book was His doing, He would have to lead me to the right publisher. I also told Him I didn't want to solicit others and do fund-raising to get the book published. Since it was His project, my expectation was that He would provide funding for it.

A dear friend made an offer to take the manuscript and get copies printed for me, but in my heart I knew that wasn't God's will. I thanked him and said I was going to wait on God. I believed with all my heart God would provide the funds to get it done professionally. Shortly after that, God directed me to a well-known self-publishing company and performed a very unique miracle of financial provision to pay for publishing!

Praise the name of the Lord! His is good and full of mercy and grace. I give God all the praise and all the glory for every single bit of this! I know there's no way I could have done any of it without Him!

I think the urgency in writing this book is because the body of Christ desperately needs a revolution in our prayer behavior. We need it to prepare us for what lies ahead. God wants the lines of communication to be fully opened between Him and every believer in the body of Christ. A narrow, ritualistic, or selfish approach to prayer is not going to be acceptable. It's a dead-end road leading to nowhere.

God is omniscient. He knows the secret things of the heart, whether spoken or not. We don't need a revolution in prayer because He is having a problem hearing us! We need it so we will be better able to hear Him and receive clear instructions of His agenda for the end times. If we don't hear Him, how can we obey?

As I said, my goal was to revolutionize our perception of prayer, so I began this book asking some questions to reveal what our current perception was. My goal was growth:

From	To
talking at God	talking with God
insecurity about whether God hears us	knowing He hears
wanting our will	submitting to His will
asking for our heart's desire	giving God our heart
cold, religious ritual	deep intimacy
fearing God's sovereignty	trusting His love
waiting in doubt and fear	waiting in confident expectation of miracles
prayer impotency	dynamic prayer potency

We are at the final process and conclusion of my assignment. Each step we took to get to this point greatly blessed me. I hope you've been blessed as well. It goes without saying that a book called *School of Prayer* cannot be complete without homework and a test. So, following this conclusion, you will find some blank pages included for your personal use:

- Appendix A   My Prayer Log
  (Record what your heart is pouring out to God.)
- Appendix B   My Prayer Journal
  (Record what God's heart is pouring out to you.)
- Appendix C   My Prayer Testimonies
  (Record miracles and answers to prayer.)

I added the appendixes because I didn't want this to be the kind of book you read or partially read, then toss aside or give away to someone else just as clean as the day you first touched it. It wanted it to be a keeper, to be written in and highlighted, with pages bent. I wanted it to be kept and referred back to later when you encountered new challenges in your prayer walk.

In addition, I don't consider this "Conclusion" as an actual end to this book. I want you to write your own personalized ending to this book by filling the blank pages of the appendixes with your personal interactions with God. Your completion of them will be the final test of whether you've learned anything or not. If you use them, I hope they will become the beginning of many future intimate journal conversations between you and God.

I've provided enough to get you started. If you've never tried prayer journaling before, it may seem a bit awkward at first. However, I guarantee you, once you get going, you'll get hooked. Before you know it, you will be out of space here and need to find yourself a new journaling notebook. May God bless you just like He did me and use journaling to help you grow in spiritual maturity in a fresh new way.

God is no respecter of persons. He's not keeping the "good stuff" for some and not for others. He has so much truth He wants to give to each and every one of us, if we will only ask, seek, and knock. He will open wide the door of revelation to His truth! In my experience, there is no way the human mind can possibly remember the depth of revelation He pours into it. You will not want to lose or forget a single bit of truth.

You will find yourself writing things down in your journal. It will be things you've never heard any teacher or preacher say before. They will be deep truths that will literally blow your mind! They will become priceless treasures you will refer back to again and again over the years. Each time you read them, they will seem just as fresh and just as helpful to get you through a new hard season, as they were when you first wrote them down.

I've been through many highs and lows in my life, but my prayer journal stands as a personal testimony to me of God's faithfulness. It is not merely a record of how God saw me through tough times. It is written proof of His unending and loving kindness. It documents how He worked all things together for my good, using both the highs and lows of my life to draw me closer to Him and transform me more into the image of Christ. It reminds me His Word of Truth will forever be a lamp to my feet and a light to my path.

I trust God will use everything you have read in this book to help you grow even closer to Him, regardless of your level of spiritual maturity. He desires all His children to experience the never-ending blessing of praying without ceasing as we walk in intimacy with Him day by day.

Closing Prayer

Magnificent Lord, God of power and might, I glorify Your holy name for You alone are perfect in mercy, righteousness, and goodness. You are love. You are truth. I thank You with all my heart for the privilege of being used by Your Spirit to write this book. Please abundantly bless all who have taken this journey with me through *School of Prayer—Time for a Revolution!*

Bless and protect the seeds of truth that have been planted in their hearts until they take root and ground each reader more deeply in Your love than they have ever experienced. In the days that follow, don't allow those truths to be stripped away by the devourer. Send forth Your laborers to water those seeds with more truth so they will grow to full maturity, and please continue to use this book in the lives of readers to transform them from glory to glory into the holy likeness of Christ.

Cause them to grow more and more in grace as they grow more and more in the revelation knowledge of Your all-encompassing love for them. Only You can bring forth the increase of a magnificent crop of Holy Spirit–empowered prayer warriors. Only You can send them forth with such an abundance of passion and power that their prayers will cover this earth with a blanket of truth and love unlike anything this world has ever known.

Dear Lord, please bind the body of Christ together in the unbreakable bond and unity of the Spirit in prayer, until we walk in Your love with such power, all will know we are Your disciples.

Keep us in that love until the day we all meet Jesus in the air to live with Him, forever.

I confidently thank You in advance for all these blessings. I know in Christ, the answer is," Yes! Amen!" They are for Your glory and praise, alone.

In Christ's holy, precious name I pray. Amen.

Maranatha!

APPENDIX A

My Prayer Log

APPENDIX B

My Prayer Journal

APPENDIX C

My Prayer Testimonies

Printed in the United States
By Bookmasters